VIDEOTEX

the new
television/telephone
information services

COMPUTING SCIENCES SERIES
Editor: S. J. Orebi Gann

VIDEOTEX

the new television/telephone information services

ROGER WOOLFE

Butler Cox & Partners Limited
London

LONDON · PHILADELPHIA · RHEINE

Heyden & Son Ltd, Spectrum House, Hillview Gardens, London NW4 2JQ, UK
Heyden & Son Inc., 247 South 41st Street, Philadelphia, PA 19104, USA
Heyden & Son GmbH, Münsterstrasse 22, 4440 Rheine, West Germany

British Library Cataloguing in Publication Data
Woolfe, Roger
    Videotex.
    1. Viewdata (Data transmisssion system)
    I. Title
    348.55'4   TK1505   80-40758

    ISBN 0-85501-493-8

Typeset in Great Britain by Computacomp (UK) Ltd, Fort William, Scotland
Printed in Great Britain by Heffers Printers Ltd, Cambridge

CONTENTS

CONTENTS

CONTENTS

FOREWORD

Computing Science has now progressed so far that it is no longer the exclusive preserve of the research specialist but extends into everyday life, from the microchip which controls the modern washing machine to a company's accounts or word-processing operations. The width, scope and impact of the subject will continue to expand during the 1980s and the purpose of this series is to chart the changes with a set of monographs and other extended works which will enable the reader to understand the effects and the potential of any key features and exciting developments in the field.

The level has been chosen to appeal to both the seasoned data processing professional who wishes to keep abreast of his subject, and to the informed layman such as the line manager, who is likely to be the end user of commercial computer systems and who wishes to appreciate the possible benefits and disadvantages in his work and even, nowadays, in his leisure activites.

This book describes the world of videotex (until recently called viewdata) systems, which is the result of linking domestic televisions to remote computers using the normal telephone network, and which provides a whole new method of information communication. Work in this field was effectively pioneered by the British Post Office which has now implemented the first large-scale public service under the name Prestel; many other countries are, however, experimenting with the idea and this book describes the benefits to both the private customer and the commercial user, and the economics of a videotex service, and then goes on to describe the worldwide plans of the national post offices.

The author is one of few people who are qualified to comment not only on the UK service but also on the worldwide developments, as much of his work during the last few years has been concentrated on monitoring closely the experiments, problems, failures and successes of the various potential service suppliers. Here for the first time is a detailed overview of the state of the videotex art at the start of the '80s.

May 1980   S. J. Orebi Gann

PREFACE

Videotex—or viewdata as it is also known—is the name of a new kind of online information service able to use adapted television receivers and suitable for use commercially or in the home.

It is already emerging as a worldwide phenomenon. In Britain, where the idea originated, the Post Office's Prestel version of videotex is already a publicly available service. Following the publicity which has surrounded its launch, Prestel is becoming increasingly visible to the man-in-the-street as well as to users in a variety of business sectors who are attracted by its ease of use and relatively low cost. Other businesses are developing their own private versions of the same basic idea.

Elsewhere in Europe many of the PTTs (state telecommunications authorities similar to Britain's Post Office) are actively developing publicly available services. They come under a variety of names: Bildschirmtext in West Germany, Viditel in Holland, DataVision in Sweden, Telset in Finland. In France there are particularly ambitious plans for videotex developments using names including Antiope, Teletel and the Electronic Directory project.

In the USA, private sector videotex plans and trials are proliferating: they have been announced by AT&T, Aregon, GTE, Knight-Ridder, OCLC and others. In Canada, almost universal allegiance to Telidon videotex technology is the common feature of trials announced by Alberta General Telephone, Bell Telephone, Manitoba Telephone System and others. And in Japan, the state telecommunications authority is testing a service called Captain with special technical features for handling the language.

The trials and service plans are marked both by similarities and differences. All share the common aim of easy use, costs appropriate for the mass market, and a range of attractive services. But the distinctions are significant; they include differences in the industries involved, in target market sectors, in specific applications, in market entry strategies, in regulatory environments and in technical features.

Now is a particularly interesting time in the history of videotex developments. The first few years of the 1980s will see videotex change from speculation and experiment to establishment as an important new medium in the residential and business marketplaces. From the foundations laid in these early years will spring the mass markets of the mid to late 1980s.

The purpose of this book is to provide a broad introduction to this fast-moving subject. The book is for readers who are not familiar with videotex, but who wish to gain a broad overview of what it is all about and where it is going. It tries to present the world scene in sufficient detail to avoid superficiality without attempting to penetrate to the level necessary for specialists. It will be of interest to a wide audience, and particularly to businessmen who want to know about videotex's potential as a medium for electronic publishing, and as a means for improving internal business communications.

December 1979   R. Woolfe

ACKNOWLEDGEMENTS

We are grateful for the co-operation of the following organizations whose illustrations are reproduced in this report:

ABC Travel Guides
British Airways
Captain Centre, Tokyo
The Caxton Publishing Company
Central Office of Information
Centre Commun d'Etudes de Télévision et de Télécommunications, Rennes, France
Consumers' Association
Department of Communications, Ottawa, Canada
Direction Générale des Télécommunications, Paris
Family Living
Information Services and Equipment Limited
ITT Consumer Products Limited
Post Office Research Centre
Prestel*
Standard Telephones & Cables

* Prestel and the Prestel symbol are trademarks of the Post Office viewdata service.

Part 1

VIDEOTEX SERVICES

the fundamentals

CHAPTER 1

VIDEOTEX INFORMATION SERVICES

WHAT VIDEOTEX IS

The term videotex

Videotex is the name of a new kind of online information service for the home, suitable for adapted TVs.

That simple statement needs some explanation and some qualification.

Online means needing a both-ways (two-way) connection—usually by telephone, though it can be by cable—to a remote computer. *Information service* is a catch phrase for a variety of services which people find useful. One such service is information retrieval: searching for and finding facts and figures stored on a computer about anything from antiques to weather reports. Another is messages which users can send to one another. And there are others.

Videotex can be used *in the home*. That means it must be inexpensive, and easy to learn and to use. It was originally conceived to make use of *adapted TVs*. Most homes have a TV and most have a telephone: put the two together, and a powerful new kind of service is created. But videotex does not have to use domestic TVs; it can use other kinds of terminal as well. Nor is its use restricted to the home. The very attributes which make it appealing in the home apply equally to businesses.

The term videotex is a generic suggested originally by the CCITT (International Telephone and Telegraph Consultative Committee). Although a definition was still being sought at the time of writing at the end of 1979, it was quite likely to include both one-way and two-way services. If that turns out to be the case, the distinction between the two service classes will probably be emphasized by calling them *broadcast* and *interactive* videotex respectively.

3

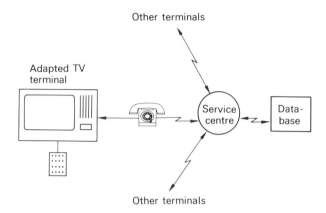

Figure 1.1. Videotex system schematic.

Purpose and scope of the book

This book is about two-way, interactive videotex. It is not about one-way broadcast videotex, though that should not be taken in any way as an indication of their relative importance. For clarity, one-way videotex, on the occasions when it is discussed here, is referred to as *teletext*. Two-way videotex is called just plain videotex from now on.

Table 1.1.   Characteristics of videotex[a]

An ability to use adapted domestic TVs as terminals.

Its appeal to a mass market rather than a small number of specialists.

Low cost, compared with traditional online information retrieval services. Videotex's relatively low cost results from its hardware/software design optimized for information retrieval; dedicated minicomputers with minimum overheads; high user loadings to reduce the system cost per user; low cost terminals; and large scale use.

Easy use, with minimal operating instructions.

An ability to be used for information retrieval, sending messages (for example, between users and information providers), computation, and software distribution.

Its display of still pages (screenfuls) of text and pictures (graphics), often in colour. Audio accompaniment and animation are both possible, though they lead to added expense.

Two-way terminal/videotex centre connections over the public switched telephone network (although two-way cable is an alternative, its use in practice is very restricted; the penetration of two-way cable is very limited, and in the public domain it is virtually non-existent).

---

[a] In the form in which the term is used in this book.

4

Table 1.1 identifies the characteristics of videotex, and Figure 1.1 is a schematic of a videotex system. Table 1.2 contains brief definitions of videotex and teletext, together with some of the other terms which are associated with services of this sort.

This book is for readers who are not familiar with videotex, but who wish to gain a broad overview of what it is all about, and where it is going. It tries to present the world scene in sufficient detail to avoid superficiality, without attempting to penetrate to the level necessary for specialists. It should be of some interest to a wide audience, and particularly to businessmen who want to know about videotex's potential as a medium for electronic publishing, and as a means for improving internal business communications.

There are three parts to the book. Part 1 is about basic principles: what videotex can do, the components of a system, who the service participants are and the likely response from the marketplace. It is generally independent of specific

Table 1.2. Videotex and associated terms

Videotex	The generic term used, but not formally approved (at the end 1979), by CCITT for a two-way interactive service emphasizing information retrieval, and capable of displaying pages of text and pictorial material on the screens of adapted TVs.
Viewdata	An alternative term to videotex, used in particular by the British Post Office and generally in Britain and the USA. Elsewhere, the term videotex is preferred. Viewdata was coined by the BPO in the early 1970s, but found to be unacceptable as a trade name; hence its use as a generic.
Teletext	A generic term used to describe one-way broadcast information services for displaying pages of text and pictorial material on the screens of adapted TVs. A limited choice of information pages is continuously cycled at the broadcasting station. By means of a keypad, a user can select one page at a time for display from the cycle.
	The information is transmitted in digital form usually using spare capacity in the broadcast TV signal. Careful design can ensure that there is no interference with the normal TV picture. Alternatively, it can use the full capacity of a dedicated channel.
	Compared with two-way videotex, teletext is inherently more limited, though generally less costly.
Teletex	A text communication standard for communicating word processors and similar terminals combining the facilities of office typewriters and text editing.
Ceefax	Ceefax ('See facts') is the British Broadcasting Company's name for its public
Oracle	teletext service available on two TV channels using spare capacity.
	Oracle ('Optional recognition of coded line electronics') is the name of the IBA's equivalent teletext service.
Bildschirmtext	The proprietary names for specific videotex implementations described in
DataVision	Part 3.
Captain	
Teletel	
Prestel	
Viewtron	
etc.	

service implementations though examples are referred to occasionally for comparison, or to illustrate a point.

Part 2 examines the background, progress to date and future plans of Britain's Prestel. As the world's first publicly available videotex service, Prestel has created worldwide interest. The experience gained with Prestel has proved useful to others intent on following a similar path.

Part 3 is about videotex plans and developments in other countries: continental Europe, the USA, Canada and Japan. The similarities—and differences—between these plans are highlighted, and the book concludes with a chapter predicting some of the ways in which videotex may change in the future.

WHAT VIDEOTEX IS FOR

Because of its two-way flexibility, videotex can be used for a variety of different things, which can be grouped conveniently under four headings: *information*

Table 1.3. Representative residential applications

Amenities and services	What's on, current events, local facilities, schools and libraries, opening/closing times.
News, sport, weather	News headlines, news summaries, local and regional news, sports fixtures and results, regional weather forecasts.
Home education	Teach yourself, home education courses, cooking, do-it-yourself, gardening, library services, hobbies, encyclopaedia, self improvement, facts and figures, general knowledge.
Welfare and consumer advice	Product and price reviews and comparisons, benefits and entitlements, shopping advice, government aid programmes.
Travel and tourism	Timetables, road conditions, sight-seeing, route planning, tours and special offers, holidays, packages.
Personal health	Diets, keep fit, recipes, exercises, medical care, self diagnosis, medical advice.
Promotion, teleshopping, classified ads	Promotional advertising, catalogue sales, classified ads, special offers.
Reservations	Hotels, planes, trains, theatres, restaurants, sports facilities.
Banking	Account balances, account transfers.
General entertainment	Quizzes and games, jokes and amusements, raffles, reviews and comments, betting.
Calculations	Tax routines, mortgage calculations, discounted cash flow, net present value.

retrieval, messages, computation, and *software distribution.* The distinction between them is not rigorous, but the aim here is to make discussion easier.

Information retrieval

Information retrieval is the term used for searching out and finding information for display on a terminal. Users select what they want to look at, a *page** (screenful) at a time, from a wide choice of possibilities. They do this either with a keypad (restricted to just numeric keys plus a few others) or keyboard (extended keypad, with keys for the letters of the alphabet) connected to the terminal. A page appears on the screen and stays there for as long as required until another one is selected or the terminal is switched off. Generally pages are still, as opposed to animated, and generally they are unaccompanied by audio, so are silent.

Some examples of the sort of information which can be retrieved in this way are timetables, news reports, classified advertisements, advice and current events. A representative list of residential applications is shown in Table 1.3.

The pages are put into videotex in the first place by *information providers.* They are responsible for the content and presentation of their pages—their accuracy, appearance, currency (keeping them up-to-date), and usually price as well. The data prepared by the information providers, and from which pages are created for display, are stored in electronic files called *databases.* Videotex users can connect with a database through a *service centre,* run by a *centre operator.* The responsibility for the whole videotex system lies with the *system operator,* who will often be a centre operator and an information provider as well.

With information retrieval, the flow of information is mainly one-way, from the service centre to users' terminals, as shown in Figure 1.2.

Messages

With a videotex message service, users (message senders) can bring specified pages to the attention of other users (recipients). Message senders can select a message page by choosing from a menu of preformatted pages such as 'happy birthday', or by creating a page by entering information themselves—for example 'I agree to your proposal' might be entered through the keyboard. Messages can be formed by a combination of selection and creation, as when a sender selects a preformatted message to confirm his intended arrival at a destination ('I will be arriving tonight at ...'), and then creates a variable part by entering the arrival time details ('19.05').

---

* Sometimes the term *frame* is used as an alternative to *page* in this book. It is likely that the authorities which recommend terms will agree definitions for page and frame, and *leaf* as well (*leaf* is not used in this book).

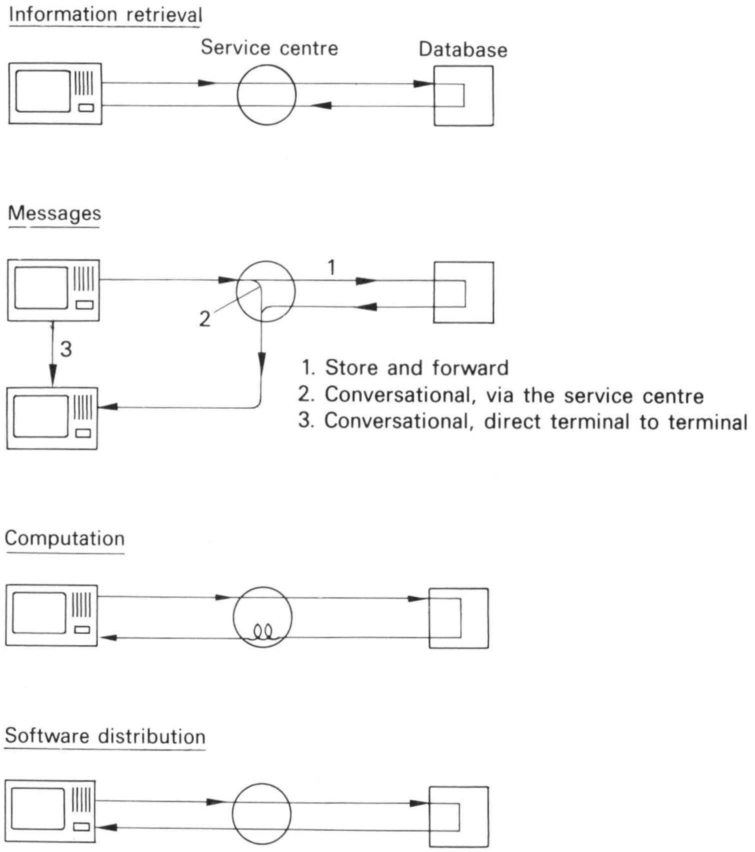

Information retrieval

Messages

1. Store and forward
2. Conversational, via the service centre
3. Conversational, direct terminal to terminal

Computation

Software distribution

Figure 1.2. Videotex information flow.

Messages can be grouped into two classes: those between ordinary users, and those between users and information providers. In both cases, messages can be sent via the videotex centre and stored there for collection by a recipient. This is called a *mailbox*, or *store and forward system*. In both types of message service, recipients are identified by a number, as with the telephone.

Sending messages may be tedious compared with the telephone, but it can be helpful when a recipient's line is busy or not answering. Messages between users and information providers are primarily for carrying out *transactions*. A user may place an order for goods to be delivered by responding to a preformatted proposal or offer page, sometimes called a *response* page. Or he may request a reservation at a hotel, or the transfer of funds between his personal checking and savings accounts at the bank. A payment mechanism may be coupled with the message, so that the acts of ordering and payment are simultaneous from the user's standpoint—called *teleshopping*.

With store and forward message services the onus is on the recipient to collect the stored message, raising a number of interesting questions about how delivery may be ensured, and who pays.

Usually messages involve storage at the service centre, though this is not essential. *Conversational* messages, which are instantaneous and involve no storage, are also possible, and are conceptually similar to the normal telephone service and to most telex systems. Either way, the flow of information in a videotex message service is backwards and forwards between users, in contrast with information retrieval (see Figure 1.2).

Computation

Computation involves data processing under a user's control at the videotex centre. Users can select what type of computation they want to carry out in much the same way as with information retrieval, and they can then enter parameters through their keypads. The programs needed to carry out the computation are stored on the database, and executed on a computer in the system. The results are transmitted back to users for display (see Figure 1.2).

An example of the sort of computation which might suit videotex is a mortgage calculation. Here a user, who could have selected a property using the information retrieval service, can respond to screen prompts (instructions) by entering parameters through the keypad to specify the interest rate, size of advance and repayment period, with the purpose of learning the value of the monthly repayments which are necessary.

Software distribution

Software distribution, sometimes called *telesoftware*, works much like information retrieval. Users specify the software item they wish to retrieve, and the corresponding pages are transmitted back to them from the centre. The distinction between information retrieval and software distribution is over the nature of the material transmitted: readable by people on the one hand, and by machines on the other.

The purpose of software distribution is to provide a rapid and convenient source of software, implying programs which are portable and standardized, and distributable on a commercial basis. An example of the use of software distribution is in programmable TV games. New games can be distributed through the telephone (*downloaded*), to be stored on a cassette, for instance. Downloading an accounting routine for running on a small business computer is another example of an application of software distribution.

SERVICE PROVIDERS AND THE MARKETPLACE

Public and private services

Videotex can be publicly available, or restricted just to private users.

Publicly available services can be aimed at either or both of the residential and business market sectors. Some information pages may be of equal interest to both, such as road conditions and travel timetables. Others will be clearly distinguishable: recipes for housewives, and commodity prices for businessmen. However, the boundaries between residential and business users are not clear cut. Many people conduct business from their homes, and businessmen often want access to leisure information from their offices. And apart from these two market sectors there are others as well. For example, terminals may be designed for use in places like airport buildings, hotel lobbies, schools and universities.

People who want to take part in a publicly available service need to have the right sort of terminal, recognizable at a videotex centre with a valid identity number. But the principle is the same as with the telephone: anyone who wants to subscribe and can afford to pay can be connected. No special membership qualifications are needed.

Private services, on the other hand, are not available to the general public. They are restricted to privileged users possessing password numbers, or equivalent identifying mechanisms. There are two broad categories of private service: *closed user group* and *in-house*.

A closed user group is a circle of users sharing a common interest. Often, the users will be geographically dispersed, such as travel agents, doctors and solicitors. Compared with a publicly available service, a closed user group service can offer added security, restricted access, and probably beneficial tariffs in return for high volume usage as well.

An in-house service is for the employees of a single business organization, and so is like a closed user group for just one company.

Private users will often use their terminals to access publicly available information. The principle of common accessibility through a single terminal is very important. The potential synergy of videotex could be realized following the adoption of its interface standards on a wide scale.

Three main service providers

To bring a publicly available service to the marketplace requires the combined efforts of three broad groups of service provider: *system operator*, *information provider*, and *terminal and equipment supplier*.

The system operator (SO) is responsible for the provision of the service centre or centres (their running may be subcontracted to a centre operator), and co-ordinating the activities of the other service providers. The SO arranges the service centre equipment and software, connection between service centres and databases, terminal connection, usage recording and subscriber billing.

SOs may be private entrepreneurial companies like newspaper publishers, computer service bureaux, or telephone companies. In Europe, where the means of telecommunications is in the hands of monopoly state controlled PTTs (postal, telephone and telegraph authorities), it is the PTTs who are the prime candidates for the SOs' role in publicly available national services. Private sector businesses, however, may compete in the provision of closed user group and in-house services.

The contents of databases are supplied by information providers—businesses seeking the attention of users, either at a fee or free of charge. To give its service broad appeal with a wide range of information topics, an SO may solicit the involvement of a number of different information providers representing, for example, general news, travel, leisure, education, local events, entertainment, consumer advice and financial news. Alternatively an SO with a limited public service, or a specialized private service, may wish to concentrate in just one area. In this case, only one information provider may be involved with an SO, such as in providing information for farmers.

Information providers choosing to become involved with videotex do so in pursuit of their normal corporate aims—profit, revenue growth, promotion, exploiting new business opportunities, or discharging an obligation to the public.

The third of the three main groups of service providers is the terminal and equipment suppliers. This group consists of TV manufacturers and retailers; semiconductor suppliers (chip sets to adapt the TVs); suppliers of computers and equipment for the service centres and databases; computer terminal suppliers; and suppliers of software and peripheral equipment.

COMPETING AND COMPLEMENTARY SYSTEMS

Because of the broad scope of the services it offers, videotex competes with and complements a number of distinct, but related services (see Figure 1.3).

Teletext is the generic term for one-way broadcast information services using adapted TVs. The information can be transmitted using spare capacity in the TV video channel. Typically a small number of pages of information—perhaps just one or two hundred—are transmitted in a continuous cycle. The restriction is due to waiting time: more pages means a longer average waiting time. For a given average waiting time, the page capacity of a teletext system can be greatly increased if the capacity of a full TV channel can be dedicated to it.

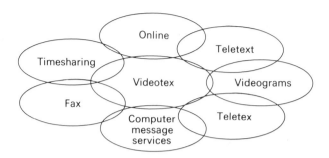

Figure 1.3. Competing and complementary systems.

Teletext users identify the page they want to see by pressing buttons on their keypads. Then they wait for the page to come round in the transmission cycle, and to be displayed.

Teletext is appropriate for topical information of general interest such as news headlines and weather reports. It avoids the expense and complication of telephone connection and the possibility of busy lines. But compared with videotex its capacity is limited, and it lacks two-way flexibility. Though they are possible with teletext, charging mechanisms are less easy to conceive and implement than with videotex, so the commercial possibilities are more restricted. However, having complementary teletext and videotex services, with heavy usage pages on teletext, is an attractive proposition.

Online information retrieval services link the terminals of subscribers to public databases (there were nearly 1000 available to European users in 1979) over two-way telephone lines or data networks. They are distinguished from videotex by being more complex, sophisticated and expensive to use. Both the users and the information tend to be specialized—for example, engineering abstracts, medical information, and company performance data.

Timesharing services offer online access to powerful computers for solving problems which need concentrated data processing power, such as in mathematical modelling and financial analysis.

With *electronic mail* users can send each other text, and sometimes graphic (picture) messages, electronically over communicating links like the telephone. Electronic mail embraces facsimile, computer message services, and communicating word processors. In Europe, the proposed standard for communicating word processors and telex in the 1980s is called *teletex*. Its aim is to promote international compatibility in the rapidly growing market for electronic mail.

The term *videogram* is a generic for TV recording systems such as video cassette recorders (VCRs) and videodiscs. As TV add-ons, videograms will compete with videotex in the residential marketplace.

This list is by no means complete. Time may reveal that the systems of the future which really compete with videotex are not even on the list. Perhaps a good example is that of automatic voice answering systems, which were making very rapid progress in the laboratories at the end of the 1970s. However, the point of the list is to show that videotex is not alone; complementary and competing services are emerging all around it.

WORLDWIDE ACTIVITY

At the end of the 1970s, videotex was being developed rapidly in many countries (see Table 1.4).

The pace-maker at this time was the British Post Office (BPO), with its Prestel product. The BPO is generally credited with the original concept of videotex, which it demonstrated in its research laboratories in the early 1970s. By 1976 it was able to start a private pilot trial with an increasing number of information providers, using TV terminals supplied by several different British manufacturers. A public market trial began in 1978, followed in 1979 by both publicly available and private closed user group services.

By the end of 1979 over 2000 terminals were attached to Prestel mainly in the London area, and the service was being expanded aggressively with more Prestel service centres due to open in London and a number of major provincial cities during 1980. The aim was for more than half the telephone-owning population of the country to be within local call reach of Prestel within about 12 months of its public service debut.

Table 1.4. Worldwide videotex activities

Country	System operator	Trial/service name
Britain	PTT	Prestel
France	PTT	Teletel, Electronic Directory
W. Germany	PTT	Bildschirmtext
Holland	PTT	Viditel
Finland	Sanoma	Telset
Sweden	PTT	DataVision
Switzerland	PTT	Videotex
USA	AT&T	Electronic Information Service
	GTE	Viewdata
	Insac	Viewdata
	Knight-Ridder	Viewtron
	OCLC	Channel 2000
	USDA	Green Thumb
Canada	AGT	Vidon
	Bell Canada	Vista
	BCT	Boris
	MTS	Ida
Japan	PTT	Captain

The BPO developed the Prestel software to run on a range of minicomputers made by GEC of Britain. With its head start, and the interest it created, the BPO was able to sell Prestel software and knowhow to other countries. The PTTs in West Germany, Holland and Switzerland all bought Prestel software and GEC computers to run the software on before the Prestel public service had started in Britain. And a company called Insac, which had negotiated the sole rights to Prestel in North America, succeeded in selling a version to GTE, the major US telecommunications company, for running on American computers.

Elsewhere in Britain, private companies were not slow to recognize the benefits of videotex for their own in-house services. Systems using the Prestel interface standard, though not the software, were running in several corporations during 1979, with more installations planned.

Other countries have developed their own videotex systems, some using the Prestel interface standards and others not. In France, the Antiope standard was developed in the mid-1970s as a basis for both teletext and videotex. Superior in some ways to Prestel, it had become an arch rival for adoption as a European standard by the end of the 1970s. The French PTT announced ambitious public service plans for the early 1980s, based on the Antiope standard. One was Teletel, offering a variety of services to the general public in a similar way to Prestel; the other the electronic telephone directory project.

Other European countries have not stood still. Apart from West Germany, Holland, Switzerland and France, two others had active development programmes underway in 1979: Finland and Sweden. Other countries had their own plans too, though they were not yet publicly announced.

In the USA, the videotex scene was characterized by proliferating private sector experiments using a variety of different software, terminal designs and standards. Over 50 independent companies, including advertisers, newspapers and travel companies, had agreed at the end of 1979 to provide information for one trial alone—Knight-Ridder's Viewtron.

In Canada, the Department of Communications (DoC) demonstrated its own system called Telidon, developed later than Prestel. Telidon features superior graphics, using techniques well known in computer-aided design. Telidon achieved wide acclaim and, with close cooperation from the DoC, was due to be tested by several Canadian system operators in the early 1980s.

Japan has also been conducting videotex experiments. Japan has had the advantage, compared with the USA, of encouragement, co-ordination and funding of its experimental activities in the field of home information services through government-sponsored bodies. But its primary interest in highly sophisticated cable systems, together with the rather cumbersome nature of the language, has led to the relatively late arrival of simple telephone-based videotex.

As one of the world's leading manufacturers of computers, terminals and TVs,

Japan's electronics industries are also acutely interested in the potential of videotex as a mass market medium.

A large proportion of this book is concerned with a closer examination of these early experiences, with the main focus of attention on publicly available services. Part 2 is devoted entirely to Britain's pioneering Prestel. Because it is further advanced in terms of installation and experience than its rivals, there is more to learn from it. Part 3 is concerned with equivalent services being developed in other countries. But before discussing these services, it is important to examine in more detail the nature of videotex system components, participants in the supply of a publicly available service, and the response of the marketplace.

CHAPTER 2

SYSTEM COMPONENTS

SERVICE CENTRES AND DATABASE ARRANGEMENTS

Service centre functions

To connect with videotex, users dial-up a service centre. It is here that a number of administration and control functions are carried out: validating subscriber, password, and closed user group numbers; storing test pages, messages, control and usage statistics, and accounting and billing data; and maintaining lists of subjects and high-level indexes.

A database of detailed indexing and information pages may also be stored at a service centre. If so, the database is *local* to the service centre. Alternatively the database may be *remote*, with the service centre acting as a gateway or switching point to the remote database, of which there may be more than one.

Private in-house and closed user group operations are usually conceived with a single service centre. Indeed, a single service centre—if it were sufficiently large—could cater for the needs of a large distributed community of, for example, residential users in a publicly available service. But this arrangement implies long distance calls, and vulnerability. The alternative is a number of smaller centres. They could be distributed in a similar way to main telephone exchanges.

The distributed service centres could be isolated from each other. In that case each could provide a specialized service, such as travel information or houses for sale. Users would connect with each centre depending on the service they wanted. But sending messages between users through the system would be difficult, and often users would be paying long distance call charges.

An alternative is to arrange for the separate service centres to be interconnected. The approach is more complex, but can be more rewarding for a publicly available service. It is this approach which is being pursued in several European countries including Britain, France and West Germany.

Designing a service centre around a minicomputer with a few hundred ports (line entry points) appears to give the most effective balance of computer equipment and transmission costs. Here each port is able to support at least one simultaneous user and, depending on its speed, often many more.

Where the average user terminal might only be expected to make infrequent use of videotex—for example, just a few minutes per day—many more terminals can be serviced than the total number of ports. This is because the probability of more than a proportion of users requiring simultaneous access is small. The challenge is to strike a balance between port loading and computer performance so that the two are adequate for most load conditions without being so generous that the economics are jeopardized.

Economic considerations require a high average port utilization, but service considerations require a high probability of port availability for a user requesting service at a random point in time. The two are in conflict. The choice of an optimal ratio of users to ports depends on a number of factors such as the average usage of each terminal, usage patterns, service economics and the desirable service level.

The target service level of the BPO's Prestel public service is over 98%. The ratio of users to ports necessary for this target to be achieved still remained to be seen at the start of the Prestel public service in 1979. BPO Prestel had earlier spoken of a ratio of around 100 residential users to each port on average, or perhaps ten typical business users, or one heavy business user.

Database arrangements

Figure 2.1 shows a single service centre arrangement with a local database, typical of test arrangements and private in-house or closed user group operations.

Figure 2.2 shows a number of isolated service centres each with its own local database. Each might specialize in a certain type of information.

Figure 2.3 shows the service centres of Figure 2.2, connected to an update centre. The databases are replicated (identical). A master database is maintained at the update centre, and changes are transmitted to the local databases. The early Prestel public service exemplifies this arrangement with information providers able to maintain their data at the update centre remotely.

Figure 2.4 shows a number of service centres connected through a network to remote databases each held on an external host computer. Users can access the information on any of the remote databases. France's Teletel plan is an example of this arrangement using the Transpac packet-switching data network.

Figure 2.5 shows a variation on Figure 2.4, with both local and remote databases. West Germany's Bildschirmtext is an example of this arrangement. Another example is that planned for Britain's Prestel, to supersede the replicated database approach.

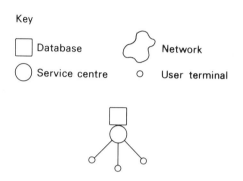

Key

☐ Database   Network

◯ Service centre   ○ User terminal

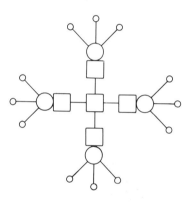

Figure 2.1.

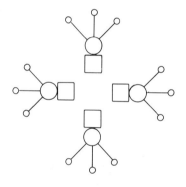

Figure 2.2.

Figure 2.3.

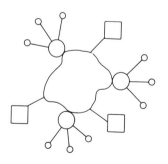

Figure 2.4.

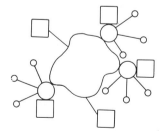

Figure 2.5.

The choice of database arrangement depends on a variety of factors, the most important of which are the strategy of the system operator, the videotex applications, the location and needs of the users, and the availability of low cost transmission links. In a publicly available service aimed at a national residential market, there are likely to be more information retrieval transactions (between users and databases) than updates (between information providers and databases). Other things being equal, it is sensible under these circumstances to arrange for databases to be as close as possible to the service centres, in order to minimize transmission costs.

A related issue concerns the form in which data should be held at the databases, and is particularly apposite to the question of using host computers. If the data are preformatted, they can be mapped on to users' display terminals with the minimum complexity. But the penalty is inflexibility. The Canadian Telidon system strives to seek independence between data and display by holding the former partly in the form of instructions, which a terminal must interpret in order to construct a display. The aim of data independence is a worthy goal, but the penalty is higher cost terminals.

Access to data by users

The goal is to provide a means of data access which is quick, cheap and easy to use. This is a major challenge, and it is by no means certain that it has been met.

That videotex should be workable by a person who is willing, and is of average intelligence but without any computer experience, is fundamental to the videotex concept. The user's need is equivalent to finding the right page in the right book on the right shelf in a bookcase. A typical videotex system will contain many thousands of information pages. This kind of scale is needed to provide the level of detail which will make the service worthwhile, even for just a limited range of topics. For a broad range of topics—as in a public service—anything less than hundreds of thousands of pages is unlikely to be enough.

Unless users can find what they want quickly, easily and inexpensively, they will be at least discouraged, and probably disillusioned. They will also want to discover in a similar way whether information they seek is not present in the system.

The key to information retrieval is the indexing method. The method widely associated with videotex during the 1970s was indexing with numbered choices. In this method, each page is uniquely numbered and the indexes are arranged in a hierarchy of increasing detail. A user works through the indexes by signifying the selection of a numbered choice through the corresponding numbered key on a keypad. The index looks like the inverted branches of a tree. Often the arrangement is called a *tree structure* (the roots of the tree are perhaps a better analogy than the branches). Figure 2.6 shows the levels of increasing refinement in a tree structured arrangement.

Another approach to indexing is the keyword method. Here each page of subject matter has one or more keywords associated with it. A separate index relates keywords to page numbers. With this method a user enters a keyword, synonym or keyword combination through his keypad, to be presented with a list of corresponding pages. By refining the keywords, the list can be reduced.

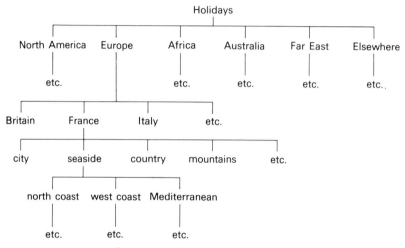

Figure 2.6.   Tree structure arrangement.

Some very sophisticated keyword searching methods have been developed, and are available with some of the specialized online information services (e.g. Lexis) which are considerably more sophisticated—and more expensive—than videotex.

A combination of keyword and numbered choice searching is also possible. The keyword method can be used as a first step, followed by indexing with numbered choices.

Another approach (used by Britain's Prestel) is to combine the use of a printed directory with the numbered choice approach. Again the purpose of the printed directory is to eliminate the early part of the numbered choice searching.

TRANSMISSION NETWORKS

Types of network

Although it is something of a simplification, Figure 2.7 indicates how three broad types of transmission network can be visualized for a videotex service: to connect users with service centres; to connect databases to service centres; and to connect information providers to databases. The characteristics required of the transmission networks are not the same.

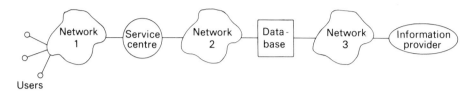

Figure 2.7.

Connecting users with service centres

The most appropriate transmission medium to connect users with service centres is the ubiquitous public switched telephone network (PSTN). Local communications between subscribers and exchanges are, with few exceptions, through copper wires designed for analogue (waveform) signals at a bandwidth (capacity) suitable for the human voice: roughly 5 kilohertz.

Although not designed for the purpose, telephone lines can also carry the digital signals needed for videotex. The digital signals can be modulated on to carrier waves by devices called modems (modulator/demodulators) at each end of the line. More precise, and therefore more expensive, modems can work at higher speeds, over longer distances, at lower error rates. As a low cost service, videotex needs low cost modems. Most videotex services under development during the 1970s were designed for transmission speeds between service centres and users of 1200 bits per second, using short haul (local call area) modems. Often the speed in the reverse direction was slower, whilst remaining fast enough to match normal keying rates, e.g. 75 bits per second (used by Prestel) is enough for about 8 characters per second.

Much higher digital data transmission speeds are possible over the PSTN, e.g. 9600 bits per second with more precise modems, often needing telephone lines to be specially conditioned by the telephone companies. But the bandwidth of the telephone network is tiny compared with that needed for broadcast TV—typically around 5 megahertz, one thousand times greater.

At 1200 bits per second it would take several minutes to transmit all the information needed to construct a broadcast TV picture frame. So videotex information is generally transmitted in shorthand using coding techniques, as explained later in this chapter.

The loading on the PSTN is typically very uneven (see Figure 2.8). At peak times in the day, coinciding with maximum business activity, the load is several times greater than the average. In some places, the peak load is already straining capacity (e.g. in parts of London). Videotex was conceived as a service for the residential market. The expectation was that off-peak telephone utilization would be improved, thus increasing revenue without the need for capital expenditure. If, perversly, videotex has the effect of adding to peak-traffic loads, some telephone companies may have to extend their capacities to cope.

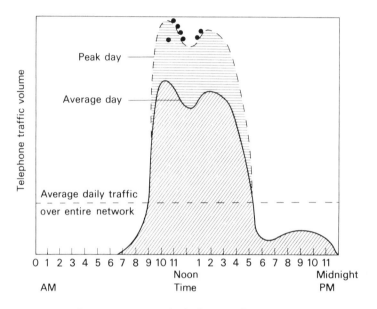

Figure 2.8. Typical telephone traffic pattern.

Connecting service centres with databases, and information providers with databases

Connecting service centres to databases, and information providers to databases, could be done using the telephone network, for example by using high capacity dedicated trunk lines.

An alternative being actively pursued, particularly in France and the USA (see Part 3), is using purpose-designed high-speed data networks based on either circuit- or packet-switching technology.

By the end of the 1970s, most European countries were actively developing public data networks of one or other type. Some were already operating, and others were due to open in the early 1980s. A common objective was to offer lower cost data transmission than with the public switched telephone network or with leased lines, particularly for intermittent users. In the USA, several *value added* packet-switched data networks were available in the 1970s with particularly attractive tariffs.

VIDEOTEX TERMINALS

The TV raster

A TV picture is formed by a fast moving electron beam which illuminates small areas of phosphor deposited permanently on the back of the screen. The beam sweeps across the screen in a succession of horizontal scan lines, each displaced below the one above. The beam starts at the top sweeping from left to right. It is switched off during the return between lines. After reaching the foot of the screen, it returns to the top to repeat the sequence.

Along each scan line, the beam illuminates colour phosphor points called picture elements (*pixels* or *pels* for short, each a colour phosphor triplet). On a typical, good quality, large colour domestic set there are about 400 to 500 pels per line. The limit of horizontal resolution is set by the TV design, the screen quality (the density of pels along a scan line) and the information carrying capacity of the broadcast picture signal.

A complete series of horizontal scan lines filling the whole screen is called a *field*. On a normal TV, the lines of alternative fields are *interlaced* to increase the vertical resolution of the resulting picture. A cycle of two interlaced fields is called a *raster*. The raster has twice the number of scan lines of a single field. In North America, a raster of 525 lines is repeated 30 times per second. In Europe, a raster of 625 lines is repeated 25 times per second. The 'persistence of vision' of the human eye—the time for which it retains an image—is slightly longer than one twenty-fifth of a second, so the eye normally gains an impression of continuity.

Interlacing the fields improves the vertical resolution, but it can also cause a flickering effect, because it doubles the time (e.g. from one fiftieth to one twenty-fifth of a second on a European TV) available for the phosphorescent image to decay.

Not all the raster lines are visible on the screen. Even in a well-adjusted set some are lost above and below the picture. Typically, a North American set shows 400 lines; a European set about 500.

So the complete TV picture is composed from a number of illuminated pels. On a large domestic TV, the number is around 250,000 (about 500 × 500; higher quality monitors can show much more—e.g. one million pels). In a colour TV the beam can cause each pel to be illuminated red, green or blue, the three primary colours.

The beam in fact consists of three separate red, green and blue signals, each of which is generated by one of three electron guns of corresponding colours (the *RGB guns*), and each of which can excite a response from the corresponding colour in a phosphor pel triplet. Six colours, together with black and white, can be mixed from these three primaries, if the intensity of each colour signal can be selected as being in either one of two states: on or off (see Table 2.1).

Further colours can be generated by varying the individual intensity of each colour signal. For example, if a third state is introduced (say half intensity), the number of colour hues increases to twenty-seven.

The text and graphic images of videotex have to be composed from illuminated pels in just the same way as the normal TV picture, as explained later.

Table 2.1.

Colour	Red	Blue	Green
Red	On	Off	Off
Blue	Off	On	Off
Green	Off	Off	On
Yellow	On	Off	On
Magenta	On	On	Off
Cyan	Off	On	On
White	On	On	On
Black	Off	Off	Off

Adapting TVs for videotex

Regular TV sets cannot display videotex—they have to be adapted using a *decoder* (sometimes called an adapter). Decoders can be fitted to TVs in the field, or during the manufacturing process. The decoder allows a TV to display text and graphics from digital signals received down a telephone line, and for information entered through a keypad to be transmitted back up the line.

Although the design of decoders differs between videotex standards, and even for the same standard, there are some common elements:

Modem, to convey digital pulses on the analogue waveform of the telephone line.
Processor, to convert incoming data into characters and graphics.
Memory, to store characters and graphics so that the TV beam can repeatedly refresh the display.
Display generator, which transfers the memory information into pel patterns, generally making use of widely available character generator electronics.
Keypad, for control and data entry.

A decoder can be fitted internally or externally to the TV. If internal (usual with Prestel) it can be wired directly to the beam circuits—that is, to the RGB guns. If external, the same can be achieved if a special RGB socket is fitted to the

TV (as planned in France). Alternatively, an external decoder can be plugged into the antenna socket (RF, for radio-frequency), but with some consequent loss in videotex display quality, particularly on colour transitions.

Fitting an internal decoder is tidier, and is often preferred by the TV manufacturing and retailing industries: it forces purchasers to trade up. External decoders allow TVs in the field to be adapted, with the potential of faster market penetration.

The modem can be integral with or separate from the decoder. Integral decoders (as with Prestel) can help reduce manufacturing costs, and demarcation problems during maintenance. Separate modems (as with Bildschirmtext) can be positioned well away from the TV, for example in the telephone handset where they can be powered from the telephone line, thus permitting the telephone company to retain both technical and price control.

There are few restrictions to the type or design of modern TV set which can be adapted to show videotex. In practice, new adapted domestic TVs for the residential market are likely to be positioned as up-market, so highly featured and with remote control. They are also likely to feature teletext, particularly where videotex and teletext share similar transmission and display standards, and there is therefore scope for sharing decoder components (as in Britain and France).

Apart from adapted domestic TVs, videotex terminals can be purpose-designed. For example, for the business market they can be designed for desk-top use. In Britain, Prestel terminals for business use need not have a broadcast TV reception capability at all. Both monochrome and colour special-purpose designs are available. Some feature full alphabetic keyboards to support a message service.

In Europe, the state monopoly PTTs restrict the attachment of devices to the public telephone network. National policies differ, but generally digital devices have to be design-approved by the PTT, and attachment must be via a PTT-supplied modem. Videotex can be an exception, however. In Britain, general approval by the BPO of a new terminal design is all that is necessary.

In practice, terminal attachment is usually via a telephone socket fitted near the TV. The TV then functions as a telephone extension when in videotex mode. To help ensure easy use, some terminal designs feature automatic dialling, and automatic terminal identification, activated by a single push button on the TV controls. Disconnection from the telephone network can also be by push button.

Non-TV terminals

Display terminals, called VDUs (visual display units), are familiar in computer installations, and to the general public in places like airline booking offices. They are unable to display videotex without modification because of differences between the two services: in line speed, character sets, protocols (rules governing how two pieces of communicating equipment communicate with one another), and display standards. VDUs cannot show broadcast TV of course, though an ability to show TV is unlikely to be a regulatory requirement of videotex. But multiple-standard terminals are a practical proposition, switchable between videotex and one or more VDU modes. By 1979, several multiple-standard designs had been demonstrated.

DISPLAYING CHARACTERS AND GRAPHICS

The display grid

Videotex characters and graphic shapes are composed by illuminating pels. This could be done by addressing separately every pel—as the TV beam does in effect when 'painting' a broadcast TV picture—but it would require a large and expensive decoder memory.

An alternative is for the display to be divided into a grid, each cell of the grid able to display a character or graphic shape from a predefined set. Then the memory capacity need only be sufficient for the contents of each cell to be defined; the beam can illuminate the corresponding pels from this information. This approach reduces flexibility, but also reduces costs. It is the approach used by Prestel, Antiope and some other videotex system designs.

Both Prestel and Antiope use a grid of 40 cells per row and 24 (Prestel) or 25 (Antiope) rows per page. A finer grid would mean more information per page, but more time waiting for the display to form while the memory fills up. It would also mean fewer pels, so poorer resolution, per character; and smaller characters are harder to read at the normal viewing distance of a TV. Forty cells per row is a compromise between these conflicting requirements. Matching this with about 25 rows per page produces character cells of an adequately balanced shape.

A key influence in Prestel's 40×24 grid choice was commonality with Britain's Ceefax/Oracle teletext, the grid for which was agreed earlier. With Ceefax/Oracle, 40 characters per row was thought to be a suitable compromise between the conflicting requirements of editing and readability. Also from a technical standpoint, it seemed about right. Britain's teletext works by encoding one character row onto one spare scan line in the TV broadcast raster. The signal bandwidth was just about sufficient for the resulting data rate to be reasonably error free. A higher rate would soon have led to unacceptably high error rates.

Other videotex systems use different grids. For example, Knight-Ridder's Viewtron uses 40×20. With the smaller number of scan lines visible on the screen of a North American compared with a European TV, accommodating much more than about 20 rows of text can present problems. And because of the more limited TV bandwidth, there are some doubts even about the desirability of 40 characters per row with RF input: 32 is sometimes favoured.

Alphamosaic displays

Prestel and Antiope are alphamosaic videotex systems: their characters and graphics are encoded for each cell, then composed in each cell from a matrix of sub-cells, called dots.

Both Prestel and Antiope use ten scan lines in a field to define each cell vertically; the 240 lines (250 for Antiope) needed in total fit comfortably into the visible area on the screen. The corresponding number of horizontal dots in the character matrix are 6 and 8 respectively: Prestel's character cell is 6×10; Antiope's is 8×10. Both cell specifications are adequate, though not generously so, to permit the generation of upper and lower case letters with some accenting, and inter-character and inter-row gaps.

1. 'Basic' 5 × 7 matrix

2. 5 × 9 matrix allowing for descenders

3. 6 × 10 character cell with inter-character and inter-row gaps

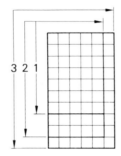

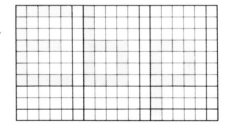

Upper case 'E', lower case 'b' and lower case 'p' formed in 6 × 10 character cells

Figure 2.9. Examples of characters defined in the basic matrix.

Figure 2.9 shows how characters can be formed from dots in a 6×10 matrix arrangement against a contrasting colour background. A 5×7 matrix (*basic matrix*) forms the body of upper and lower case characters. Two additional rows of dots form descenders for the lower case letters g, j, p and q. Inter-character and inter-row gaps are one dot wide.

In some terminal designs a technique called *half-shift enhancement* is used to help round the shape of the characters. The dots on the scan lines of alternate fields are shifted horizontally by a half position with respect to one another, smoothing the changes in dot position between adjacent scan lines.

Several *attributes* can be defined for each individual character, in order to enhance the flexibility and attractiveness of screen presentations. For example

foreground/background colour
flashing or steady
single or double height.

With alphamosaic videotex systems, graphics are formed in a very similar way to characters—from elemental shapes formed within the cells from a coarse matrix of dots. Attributes can be defined for graphics just as for characters.

If the same number of dots were used as with character formation, the number of possible combinations in a cell (which would include of course all the characters) would be impractically large: for Prestel's 6×10 matrix, it would be 2^{60}.

An alternative is to use a coarser dot matrix for graphics. Both Prestel and Antiope do this, dividing each cell into a 2×3 dot matrix to give 2^6, i.e. 64 combinations per cell, as shown in Figure 2.10.

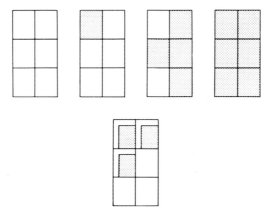

Figure 2.10.   Coarse 2×3 graphic dot matrix.

The figure shows how the resulting graphic dots are approximately square (there is some asymmetry between them in the vertical direction to accord with the 10 available scan lines). It also shows how *separated graphics* can be achieved by reducing the size of each graphic dot (by the width of a dot used in character formation), in both horizontal and vertical planes.

It is the coarseness of the graphic dots which gives both Prestel and Antiope their rather granular—or mosaic—appearance. A measure of their graphics resolution is the total number of graphic dots which can be resolved. With Prestel this is 80 horizontally (40 cells per row, 2 graphic dots per cell), and 72 vertically (24 cells per column, 3 dots per cell)—a total of about 6000. This compares with about a quarter of a million pels in a typical TV video picture.

One way to improve on this relative coarseness is by increasing the number of graphic dots per cell, but that means a larger number of possible combinations which have to be encoded, unless the range is restricted just to a limited selection of combinations.

Another very practical alternative is called DRCS—*dynamically redefinable character sets*. The idea is that sets of additional characters can be defined from any combination of dots in the character matrix, and downloaded to the terminal. This can be done as required, if necessary for every page, though there is an overhead penalty each time a new DRCS is loaded. The benefit of DRCS is that the technique can be used to extend the character set to any possible combination of dots in the cell matrix, so long as just a limited selection is used on a given page. The extended character set can of course contain special symbols and graphic shapes of all sorts.

There is another, entirely different, approach to the problem of coarse graphics. This is to avoid encoding combinations of dots in a graphic cell. Rather, the dots can be transmitted and stored individually, then mapped on the display in a way reminiscent of facsimile.

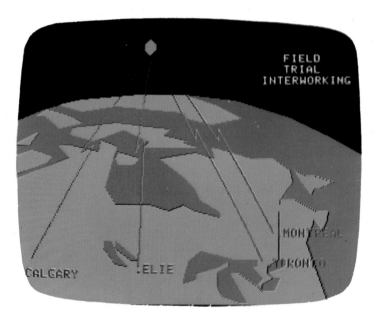

Figure 2.11. Example of a Telidon display.

This method of mapping dots directly on to the display is sometimes called the *frame store* or *bit map* approach, to distinguish it from the *character generation* method described above. The frame store concept opens the door to improved graphics resolution. Ultimately, each pel on the TV screen might be a graphics dot. The penalty is increased transmission and storage requirements.

Alphageometric and alphaphotographic displays

A way of circumventing the transmission problem is for the task of graphics generation to be undertaken in the terminal from instructions which are encoded and transmitted. When coupled with character generation as already described, the approach is called *alphageometric*.

The alphageometric method is exemplified by Canada's Telidon. Here, drawing commands are transmitted using picture description instructions (PDIs). Telidon uses just a few types of PDI, each defining a basic shape such as line, circular arc and polygon. The resulting graphic shapes can be displayed over a large screen area. A major advantage is that the graphics instructions are independent of terminal resolution. The logic in each receiving terminal interprets the instructions as best it can. The picture resolution is determined not by the data but by the terminal—in practice mainly by its memory capacity (see Figure 2.11).

Early Telidon terminals were demonstrated with an ability to store about 50,000 dots, and to resolve them separately on the display. With larger memories, Telidon terminals could improve this resolution without changes to the database.

Of course, the geometric approach to graphic formation is limited to those shapes which can be specified geometrically without much difficulty. There is a surprisingly wide range of shapes which can be assembled from basic graphical primitives. But the procedure can get complicated, and ultimately is limited.

Alphaphotographic is the term used to describe the technique in which every dot is transmitted separately to construct a shape. The approach is closely related to facsimile, and slow-scan TV. It removes the restrictions of the alphageometric approach, but at the expense of transmission time and cost.

Alphamosaic, alphageometric and alphaphotographic methods can all be used in combination on a single page. Indeed, Telidon was able to demonstrate this ability as early as 1978, with a restricted photographic display area resulting from the limited internal memory capacity of the terminals available at the time.

Readability of text and acceptability of graphics

Television was not designed with the readability of displayed text as a primary consideration. The key factors which condition the readability of text from a TV screen are to do with the physical properties of the display itself, the presentation of the information on page, and the positioning of the terminal with respect to the user.

The physical properties of the display are set by factors such as character size and shape, character spacing, stability, colour, brightness and contrast. Prestel's 6 × 10 character dot matrix is acceptable for characters in the English language, but it is barely acceptable for other Latin-based languages involving accenting, and unacceptable for many non-Latin-based languages. The position would be greatly improved by increasing the number of scan lines (i.e. vertical dots) allocated per cell. A variety of alternatives have been proposed. For example, 14 scan lines would allow 2 extra scan lines above the basic matrix for accenting upper case letters, and 2 extra below for underlining and for improving the inter-row spacing. The penalty with proposals of this sort is that they further restrict the already limited display capacity.

This illustrates the room for manoeuvre which exists with just one aspect of character size and shape. Other factors include character spacing, stability, colour, luminance and contrast. The interrelation of these factors is a design study in itself, and beyond the scope of this book. But what is clear from research carried out during the 1970s is that subtle differences in these factors can lead to large differences in readability.

The presentation of the information on a page is also very influential in determining readability. The restricted capacity of the videotex page means that designers' skill and imagination are even more important than on larger capacity displays. Clarity and simplicity are both very important. The Prestel examples in Figure 2.12 are an apt illustration of this (the experience of Prestel information providers in this area is summarized in Chapter 8).

The positioning of the terminal is important in that it dictates factors such as glare and reflections, together with viewing angle and the distance of the screen from the eye. Domestic TVs are not usually viewed under the more highly controlled lighting conditions usually associated with VDUs. When broadcast programmes are viewed, this may not matter, but for videotex, normally acceptable TV viewing conditions may be quite inadequate. How important a deterrent this will turn out to be remains to be seen. If the majority of residential use is casual or intermittent, it may not be a serious problem.

Besides altering its appearance, the inclusion of graphics in a videotex page can materially affect understanding, for example by reinforcing a title to make its meaning more immediately apparent, or by conveying complex information as with a graph or histogram. Sometimes the clarity of a graphics message is very dependent on fine resolution—as with a map. At other times, the need for fine resolution is much less obvious.

However, there is little doubt that graphic pictures with fine resolution have a greater appeal than those without. On most occasions when alphageometric or

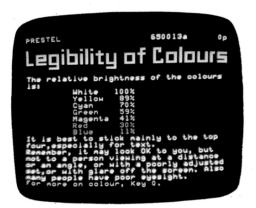

Figure 2.12. Prestel examples of page design.

alphaphotographic displays have been demonstrated alongside alphamosaic displays, the former have created a more favourable impression. At the end of the 1970s, it was still not clear just how important and longlasting this impression would turn out to be.

CHARACTER SETS AND CODES

7-bit codes

Several hundred unique characters are required by the Latin-based languages to cover the requirements of upper and lower case alphabetics, accented characters, punctuation marks, symbols and numerals.

Prestel examples of page design—*contd.*

Standards for transmitting digital information over the PSTN are laid down by ISO—the International Standards Organization. The standard for codes using 7-bit characters is ISO 646, the same as CCITT Recommendation V3. It is very closely allied to ASCII.

Seven bits gives 128 combinations ($2^7 = 128$). The 128 unique combinations are normally represented as a code table consisting of 8 columns and 16 rows, with each cell in the table represented by its column and row number (see Figure 2.13).

The code table is partitioned into two areas, the control (C) and graphics (G) sets. The C set is defined in the first two columns of the code table, and the G set in the last six columns. Thus 32 of the 7-bit codes are reserved for control characters, leaving 96 codes for characters for display. Two of these 96 are

33

reserved for the space character (table position 2/0), and the delete character (position 7/15).

For the English language 94 codes are sufficient to define the upper and lower case alphabetic characters, the ten numerals, and a reasonable selection of punctuation and other special symbols. But 94 characters are not sufficient for languages which make use of accents (e.g. French and German), particularly if each accent/character combination is treated as a separate character. The CCITT/ISO standards recognize that 94 characters are not sufficient, and permit code extension so that several interpretations can be given to the same 7-bit code.

The basic G set is called the G_0 set. The alternative interpretations are defined as additional G sets, called the G_1, G_2 and G_3 sets. Code extension is achieved by

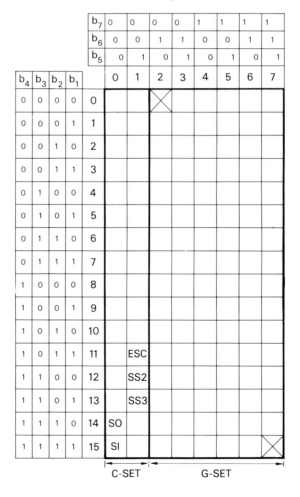

Figure 2.13.　The basic 7-bit code structure.

switching between different G sets by the use of special control characters, the most important of which are shown in Figure 2.13 and are:

ESC = Escape
SO = Shift out
SI = Shift in
SS2 = Single shift 2
SS3 = Single shift 3

When transmission begins, a terminal interprets the 7-bit G set codes as per the G_0 set. When an SO control code is received, the terminal switches to the G_1 set, until an SI code is received, when it reverts to the G_0 set. When an SS2 (or SS3) control code is received, the terminal switches to the G_2 (or G_3) set for the next character only (see Figure 2.14).

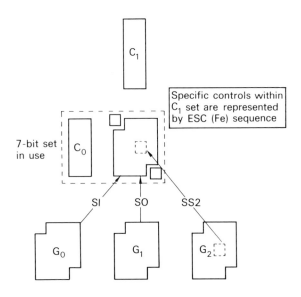

Figure 2.14. Principles of code extension.

Alternative C sets can also be defined, and these are accessed by using the ESC control code.

Prestel and Antiope compared

Both Prestel and Antiope are similar in concept and have many common features. However, there are a number of detailed differences in the way in which some of the features are implemented (see Table 2.2).

Table 2.2. Prestel and Antiope: similarities and differences

		Prestel	Antiope
Similarities	625 line raster	√	√
	alphamosaic	√	√
	40 characters/row	√	√
	6 colours, black and white	√	√
	similar character attributes	√	√
	7-bit transmission	√	√
Differences	character memory size	8 bits	16 bits
	character attributes	serial	parallel
	character coding	direct	composite
	rows per page	24	25

The main differences are due to the amount of memory which is used to store the 7-bit codes transmitted to the terminal. Prestel uses an 8-bit memory for each character, whereas Antiope uses 16 bits.* Thus Prestel can store only one additional bit of information with each 7-bit code, whilst Antiope terminals can store 9 additional bits.

Antiope terminals are therefore able to store most of the character attributes with each individual character (*parallel coding* of attributes). With Prestel terminals, character attributes are defined for a string of characters (*serial coding* of attributes), by storing one or more control characters in the terminal memory. These control characters occupy a memory position allocated to a display character cell, and are displayed on the screen as spaces (sometimes referred to as 'black holes'), unless they are deliberately covered up by *holding over* (repeating) the graphic content of the immediately preceding character cell.

With Prestel it is not possible to display two consecutive alphanumeric characters in different colours. A control character specifying the colour change has to be present between the two characters, and this will be displayed as a space. Antiope terminals can vary (most of) the attributes of consecutive characters, since the attributes form an integral part of each character stored in the terminal's memory.

Other detailed differences between Prestel and Antiope are the use of a 25th row by Antiope, and the way in which double height characters are formed (on Antiope terminals, extension is upwards to the previous row; on Prestel terminals, it is downwards to the next row). Antiope terminals also use character attributes not available on Prestel (double width characters, and specific setting of black as a background colour).

---

* 16 bits is normal for Antiope, though terminals with more (e.g. 20) and less (e.g. 8) have also been demonstrated.

Figure 2.15. Example of an Antiope display.

The standardization debate

There are obvious advantages if a common worldwide videotex standard can be agreed. Standardization should lead to confidence amongst service suppliers. Larger production volumes should lead to lower prices. And international standardization should facilitate international use.

A major part of the European videotex standards debate has been about the method for coding special characters and, in particular, accented characters. The Antiope standard uses a *composite* character coding technique where the accent mark and character to be accented are transmitted as two separate 7-bit codes. CCITT standards require that a backspace character is also transmitted between the accent and alphabetic character. The terminal recognizes the string of characters, and constructs a composite character for display in the appropriate character cell.

The accent mark is coded in a G_2 set, and four characters need to be transmitted to create an accented lower case character as shown by Figure 2.16.

The Antiope standard for accented characters discussed in 1979 was closely compatible with the coding scheme for the proposed teletex (super telex) standard which seemed likely to be adopted by CCITT in 1980. Many of the PTTs involved in formulating the teletex standard believed videotex/teletex compatibility to be an important consideration.

37

At the same time Prestel did not display accented characters; it did not have a need to do so, since the English language does not require them. However, in 1978 and 1979 the British Post Office made proposals to extend the Prestel standard to include the requirements of all languages, so that Prestel could form the basis for an international videotex standard. Prestel was closely tied to the British teletext standard and, in making their proposals, the BPO were anxious not to make obsolete the existing Prestel and teletext terminal population (Britain was then the only country to operate a public service for either type of system).

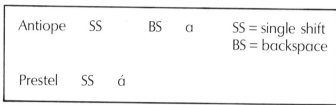

Figure 2.16.   Creating accented character 'á'

The BPO proposed a *direct method* of coding accented characters (compared with the composite Antiope method described earlier). The proposal was for each individual accent/character combination to be allocated a separate 7-bit code in a G_2 or G_3 set. Thus different code table positions would be allocated for 'a' and 'á'. The advantage of the direct method of coding is that it is more efficient, since only two 7-bit codes have to be transmitted in this example, as shown by Figure 2.16.

The British proposals met with strong resistance from other European PTTs, so the BPO was forced to change its position. During the summer of 1979, it presented alternative proposals to CEPT (the European PTTs' trade association), which appeared to be acceptable bases for a compromise videotex standard for Europe.

Eventually, the BPO agreed that composite coding for accented characters was acceptable. This concession was made because the BPO realized it would never have to implement it in Britain, where accented characters are not required. The main features of the emerging compromise standard were:

each country could use its own version of the G_0 set
character attributes could be coded in a serial or parallel way, thus permitting 8- or 16-bit memories
each country could use C sets specific to its own videotex implementations
terminals could assume default G and C sets specific to the country in which they were being used, but would be capable of receiving instructions to change the G and C sets currently in use.

The intention was to ensure the upwards compatibility of this proposed standard with both existing British and French videotex developments. If a terminal in one country were used to access a foreign videotex system using different C and G sets, the host system would first transmit to the terminal details of the C set to be used. The details of precisely how this might be achieved were still being worked out at the time of writing.

Some interesting consequences would arise if the compromise proposals were adopted. Antiope terminals accessing a Prestel database would always be able to display information in exactly the same way as Prestel terminals. For the reverse situation this would not be true, and some Antiope information would be lost when displayed on Prestel terminals. The way in which attributes are coded means that a 40 character row for display on an Antiope terminal could create more than 40 characters when converted to a Prestel compatible format. Also, Prestel terminals cannot use the 25th row available on Antiope terminals. In effect, the proposed compromise standard would make Prestel a sub-set of Antiope.

Both Prestel and Antiope, in their basic forms, are alphamosaic systems. Future developments of videotex may well be alphageometric or alphaphotographic, to gain the advantages of enhanced graphic displays. Any first generation alphamosaic standard which might be agreed should benefit if conceived as a sub-set of a future frame store standard. This way, later generation standards could be upwards compatible from earlier generations.

CHAPTER 3

PARTICIPANTS IN THE SUPPLY OF A PUBLICLY AVAILABLE SERVICE

SYSTEM OPERATORS AND THE PTTs

System operators' interest in videotex

System operators are responsible for providing videotex services. A system operator co-ordinates the activities of the other service participants, and is responsible for marketing and subscriber contact, and for the commercial foundation of the service. Typically, system operators will run the videotex service centres themselves, and may be involved with information provision and the supply of terminals as well.

For publicly available services in Europe, the system operators are the PTTs (Postal, Telephone and Telegraph authorities), the monopoly suppliers of telephone services. Their control over the means of communication makes them natural candidates for the role. Although in the past their prime concern has been in the area of 'traditional' telecommunications, they have been interpreting their monopoly charters more liberally in recent years. Their enthusiasm for videotex is an example of this. Through their monopoly positions, and the availability of state capital (albeit carefully controlled), they are in a strong position to expand their videotex interests rapidly. How their roles might be regulated is a subject of intense discussion in many European countries, as explained in Part 3.

In Europe, private sector companies may also be system operators. They could, for example, provide private closed user group services unless they involve switching messages between private subscribers, which may be construed to contravene a PTT's monopoly. PTTs permitting private services to flourish may find it hard to decide the point when they become effectively publicly available, and what to do about it if they do. In the future, there may be a number of videotex services available to a European terminal owner, with PTTs and private sector industry system operators competing for attention.

In the USA, private sector system operators can offer videotex in competition with similar services in the database and electronic mail areas. Although the regulatory position was still unclear at the end of 1979, relative freedom from regulatory constraints was likely at least in the short term (see Chapter 12). Potential system operators include newspaper companies (like Knight-Ridder), TV and electronics companies (like RCA), and telephone companies (like GTE).

What motivates the potential suppliers of publicly available videotex services is the prospect of profit and revenue growth from a mass market operation. This remains the goal, even though the means of achieving it may differ. For example, system operators and information providers are primarily concerned with terminal usage; the TV industry with terminal sales. The telephone companies in particular are interested in increasing the utilization of the telephone network, as explained in Chapter 2. And the PTTs are particularly interested in positioning themselves for the future, when they hope to exploit the long-heralded information explosion in homes as well as businesses.

Strategies for mass market creation

The interest of the major corporations in videotex, and certainly the PTTs, stems from its mass market potential in a publicly available service. But service prices are volume sensitive; the larger the volume the lower the unit price. At mass market volumes, prices could be low enough—just—for mass market acceptance. But at lower volumes prices will remain too high (unless subsidized), except for less price-sensitive markets. This is the classical conundrum. What strategies can suppliers adopt to create a mass market?

One is to target a less price-sensitive market sector at first, such as a defined business sector or geographical area, and to build from there.

Another is to grow the market as quickly as possible by offering a nationwide service with a wide range of topics. The heavy investment and high risk for the system operator is countered by the prospects of a relatively early pay back. The British Post Office's Prestel is an example of this approach (see Chapter 5).

Another is to stimulate the market by supplying equipment such as decoders free of charge. The French PTT plans to provide free terminals in its electronic directory project as explained in Chapter 11.

A further question for system operators is whether to embark on videotex now, or to wait. The expectation is that in the future the price of technology will fall, levels of disposable income will continue slowly to rise, and the cost of labour intensive information services, such as newspapers and letterpost, will rise rapidly. On the other hand, competitors to videotex will become better established.

System operators choosing to develop public videotex services now, such as the European PTTs, will have taken account of these conflicting pressures.

THE INFORMATION PROVIDERS

Publishing

Videotex is a new way for industries involved with information to provide their customers with services. Many industries are potential information providers, and they are actively examining the potential of videotex. They include publishing, marketing, travel and tourism, online services, banking and credit operations, education, government and leisure.

It is the publishing industry which has reacted most strongly to videotex. About 35 publishing information providers (called IPs in Britain) were participating with Prestel at the start of its public service. Elsewhere in Europe there was a similar degree of interest. And in West Germany the publishing industry's enthusiasm for Bildschirmtext was almost overwhelming. In the USA, Canada and Japan, publishing companies were well represented amongst information providers in the early trial plans (see Part 3).

In general the industry does not see videotex as an immediate threat to existing publications, but rather as an alternative medium suitable to complement them. Videotex is seen as a forerunner of other new media expected in the longer term, and able to substitute at least some part of the existing media. For publishers, videotex also represents an opportunity to enter new markets and provide new types of service.

The traditional publications most likely to feel videotex's impact are those which it can most easily complement or substitute. These are the types of publication where videotex's special attributes—high momentary value, and compact up-to-date presentation—apply most easily.

Thus the printed publications most likely to be threatened can be identified. An example is summarized material of high spot value not requiring high quality illustrations, for example news letters, guides, advice sheets and fact sheets. Another is reference and catalogue material, for example directories and timetables. A third is compact and volatile data, such as classified advertisements.

Conversely, the print products least likely to be threatened are those which are descriptive or lengthy, for which portability and high quality illustrations are important, and which contain information of generally low volatility.

Newspapers contain a mix of information, some of which is suitable for videotex, like 'what's on', horoscope, news summary and classified advertisements; and some of which is less suitable, such as opinion and editorial comment. Newspapers, particularly local newspapers, could be complemented by videotex. Newspapers have the skills and organization needed for material collection, condensation and presentation. It is no surprise that they are showing such active interest in videotex.

Marketing

The marketing industry, which includes commercial advertising, direct selling and market research, is another candidate for exploiting videotex.

While videotex's graphic quality remains limited, as with the basic Prestel and Antiope systems, its use in promotional advertising will remain restricted. Its lack of sound and movement put it at a disadvantage compared with promotion, where that is permitted, through regular TV channels. And there are doubts in some countries over the extent to which promotion on videotex will be permitted.

For direct selling, videotex has the great advantage of convenience. A user's ability to place an order through the system will be important, particularly in conjunction with regular TV promotion. The ability simultaneously to effect a purchase transaction, with a credit card number or by direct debit, will allow sales to be closed very conveniently.

A major attraction to market researchers, once a full public videotex service is established, will be the prospect of statistics on page viewing, which could provide a level of market research detail never before available.

Travel and tourism

The response of the travel and tourism industry to videotex has been particularly favourable in Britain, and has met with growing interest elsewhere. There are three main areas of interest.

The first is as a means of improving travel agents' access to current information to help them provide their customers with a better service. For example, videotex can provide up-to-date travel information such as schedules, timetables, seat availability, fares and special offers.

The second is as a means of bringing travel and tour information to business and residential users in order to increase their awareness of services—for example, holidays, discounts, tours, fares and special offers. This is essentially a promotional activity.

The third is to permit videotex users to make their own travel plans and reservations directly from their homes and offices. Although this is a serious threat to part of their business, a common view amongst travel agents is that they will always be needed to provide the kind of personal service—such as advice and venue selection—which no automated system can provide.

Banking

The banking community's interest in videotex lies in its potential for disseminating information, and for electronic funds transfer (EFT).

Information dissemination applications could be both external (to home users) and internal (between branches). Of these the former will be more important, and could provide users with the ability to view details such as their account balances and recent account movements.

At a later stage customers could gain access to their own accounts, and could use the message service as a means, for example, of ordering cheque books and transferring funds between different personal accounts. Conceivably banks could enter closed user group videotex networks offering information to, for instance, real estate agents about mortgages, or even giving them facilities for banking transactions—though this would require a careful review of privacy and security issues.

But the banks' main interest in videotex lies in its potential for EFT. Its use for credit card purchasing is a promising application area, particularly for mail order company products. Another possibility in Europe is for videotex to provide savings bank customers with the means to enter their Giro transfers through home terminals, in order to disperse the data capture process and reduce handling costs.

In the USA the potential for home banking terminals is enormous, for two key reasons. First, banks (unless they are foreign-owned) are prevented from providing out-of-state branch services. Internal state restrictions apply as well, which can constrain the number of branches in a town. Second, the banks are required to keep a proportion of their account values in the Federal Reserve System (FRS) as a kind of insurance premium. But telephone account services, such as bill paying, are not required to be reflected in this proportion.

The availability of home terminals would help the banks spread into new state territories, and, by supporting the spread of telephone-based services, could help reduce the banks' FRS deposits.

Education

In formal education, videotex could play a useful role as a self-contained teaching system, as an illustrative medium, and for providing low cost access to general computing facilities.

In informal education there are several candidates for early videotex applications, including private education, skills teaching for office and industry, home-based adult education, access to other databases, course choice and career guidance, and as the means of transmitting educational software for use in personal computers.

Other information providers

Another important potential information provider, particularly in Europe, is the government. Government agencies are interested in low cost systems for mass information dissemination, and to help the business community and the public at large to access an increasing amount of government data.

The interest in videotex of the industry sectors described above is not always the same, and each can see discouraging as well as encouraging aspects to their involvement. The more important of these conflicting factors are summarized in Table 3.1.

Table 3.1. Factors influencing information providers' involvement with videotex

Encouraging involvement
   Profit from frame accesses by direct frame sales or indirectly through the sale of related products.
   Cost reduction by reducing expensive alternative information forms (e.g. as with the French PTT which plans to reduce the cost of telephone enquiry services following its introduction of an electronic telephone directory service).
   Learning opportunity with a new medium—important for the future 'less paper' society.
   Instant feedback about individual frame usage (which can readily be collected in terms of gross frame accesses in a period, though not necessarily itemized by individual user to preserve both privacy and economics).

Discouraging involvement
   Investment risk.
   Uncertain applications. There is still considerable uncertainty about which applications will prove to be popular in the long term.
   New unexplored territory, unfamiliar even to IPs with experience, e.g. in the online database marketplace.
   Copyright and security issues concerned, for example, with information ownership, enforcement and security against unauthorized access from other users and other IPs.
   Need for new design skills both for database design and for individual page design. Research has indicated that these design areas present new challenges requiring new approaches for solution.
   Ongoing frame maintenance commitment. IPs unable or unwilling to keep their information pages up-to-date risk damaging their reputations.
   Visual limitations, resulting from the limited typographic capability of present generation videotex systems, limited colour ranges and limited graphics for pictorial representations.
   Need for heavy promotion to create awareness. Although the key promotional point is the TV retail store, IPs (and SOs) will need to be involved with promotion as well as the TV industry in order to create awareness and a sense of need amongst potential buyers in a general sense—and IPs will have to be concerned with promoting their individual videotex frames in a specific sense.

THE TV, EQUIPMENT AND SOFTWARE INDUSTRIES

TV manufacturers

In most Western countries the markets for colour TVs are approaching saturation, with annual sales well down on the peaks of the 1960s and early 1970s. Profits have been tight and competition fierce, exacerbated by imports from Japan.

Added to that, the life expectancy of TVs has been increasing. The industry is looking for new products and new markets to carry it through the 1980s.

To this industry, videotex holds the promise of a mass market for replacement TVs of higher added value for the residential market. It also offers prospects for the industry to break into the business market, and into new markets such as TV terminals in schools, institutions and public places. But although the prospects look exciting, the industry is aware of potential pitfalls.

Videotex is primarily about information, not entertainment. This is a realm with which the industry is not familiar, unlike the established terminal and office equipment industries. It involves new partnerships, for example with the telephone companies and information providers.

It also poses a problem of standardization. In Europe, the prime contenders for adoption as a standard have been Britain's Prestel and France's Antiope, as explained in Chapter 2. At the end of the 1970s they were not compatible, though strenuous efforts were being made to arrive at a compromise between them. Elsewhere, other standards have been strongly promoted such as Canada's Telidon which has achieved wide international acclaim.

But the greatest potential obstacle confronting the TV industry's involvement with videotex is the emergence of alternative investment opportunities. Most attractive to the industry are the new opportunities in its traditional field of entertainment. They include VCRs for time-shift recording of broadcast TV, and later for playback of home telecine; videodisc for low cost playback of pre-recorded video material; better TV games; and projection screen equipment.

At present these are add-on products which do not necessarily require users to change their TVs. But new TVs are designed with these enhancements in mind, so work better with them. And they offer other enhancements too, aimed at improving quality, reliability and ease of use. The TV industry will find it hard to back all these new opportunities simultaneously.

Semiconductor suppliers

The semiconductor industry has seen mass markets develop for its chip sets in calculators, watches and TV games, measured in hundreds of millions. Its attention is now focused on new market areas, including consumer durables such as automobiles and kitchen equipment, office equipment, and capital equipment such as manufacturing plant controls.

The TV itself is a candidate for microprocessor control, even in the absence of videotex. However, both teletext and videotex are attractive new market opportunities. Both offer the mass market potential which is sought after by the semiconductor industry.

The industry is looking to the TV manufacturers to place the large scale orders which will result in low unit costs.

Computer equipment and software

Videotex presents an opportunity to the established computer equipment and software industries to supply videotex centres, terminals and database-supporting external computers for both public and private operations.

The main opportunity in computer hardware is with dedicated minicomputers optimized for information retrieval and fast switching, and generally in the size range from a few ports up to 200 or more.

For the traditional terminal equipment suppliers, videotex's advent could open up an opportunity to provide new types of terminals. There is likely to be a need for VDUs able to access both regular and videotex databases, with the opportunity to take advantage, wherever appropriate, of low cost modems. Another opportunity will be for TV-based terminals in competition with the TV industry. They will be aimed at the business market, where the terminal equipment suppliers are better established.

For the software industry, videotex presents opportunities both for supporting service centre operations, and for software distribution. Software for service centre operation presents a significant challenge. Though the basic videotex software is essentially quite simple, the software for a full public service can be extremely complex. And software to be stored on videotex databases and distributed by downline loading presents an entirely different, and just as demanding, challenge. It must be compact, portable and standardized, often containing routines to permit vendors to rent the software, and then to terminate the rental after a defined time period or on a specified date.

INVESTMENT AND RETURNS

System operators

Videotex's prospects as a commercial venture rest on its ability to provide the service suppliers with a reasonable return on their investments. In high price market sectors there is no doubt about its ability to achieve this, so long as there is a demand for the service. But can it achieve the same in the lower price, higher volume mass market for which it was conceived? To help answer this question it is necessary to make a number of assumptions.

Consider a 300 port videotex service centre with 250,000 pages of information, servicing a population of 30,000 residential users (100 per port). 300 ports loaded for 5.5 hours, 300 days per year, gives about 500,000 port hours per year. Assuming a page access rate of one every 15 seconds, this gives a capacity for 120 million page accesses per year at the service centre.

Assume the cost of a service centre, inclusive of hardware depreciation, software, operating staff, consumables, real estate and overheads, to be about $1 million per annum.

What connect-time rate will have to be charged to pay off this total cost of $1 million per annum? An average rate of $2 per port hour will just equal the total running cost ($1 million and 500,000 port hours). A rate of 4 cents per minute—equivalent to $2.4 per port hour—generates a total revenue to the system operator of $1.2 million, sufficient to provide a small return on investment.

Information providers

In addition, the information providers' costs must be covered by revenues which users should be willing to pay, over and above the connect-time charge. Information providers' costs for preparing and maintaining pages of information will vary greatly according to factors such as the cost of data collection, the complexity of page designs, and the frequency of updating.

Assume a typical all-inclusive page cost to be $40 per year. To recover this cost, and make a return on investment, an information provider will look for gross revenues of at least $60 per page per year. The single videotex service centre with a capacity of 120 million accesses per year yields an average number of accesses to each of its 250,000 pages of 480. Although the concept of an 'average access' frame is somewhat unreal, the 480 accesses will only yield the necessary $60 at an average charge per access of over 12 cents—too high for a mass market to bear.

But the single videotex centre only supports a population of 30,000. The key to videotex's service economics lies in extending the user base. With the same selection of pages available at ten videotex centres rather than one, the cost of accessing the average page falls to one tenth of 12.5 cents, i.e. 1.25 cents—a much more acceptable figure.

With this model, a typical user would pay 4 cents per minute for connect-time to the database, and 1.25 cents per average page. The user viewing four pages per minute would be paying around 9 cents per minute for the service, excluding telephone and TV terminal costs.

The figures for port hours and total users per service centre yield an average of 20 minutes per user per week. That is equivalent to about 80 pages of information, at a cost for connect-time and page accesses of about $1.80.

Telephone charges will vary greatly, for example according to time of day and distance. Assume a rough average to be 2 cents per minute. Users can also expect to pay for their adapted TVs. Assume the premium price of a new adapted TV to be $200, equivalent to around $50 per annum.

Thus a typical home videotex user might spend around $160 per year:

connect-time to the videotex centre	$40
frame access charges	$50
telephone connection	$20
adapted TV	$50
	$160

The gross revenue generated per videotex centre supporting a population of 30,000 residential users will be just under $5 million:

connect-time to the centre	$1.2 million
frame access charges	$1.5 million
telephone connections	$0.6 million
adapted TVs	$1.5 million
	$4.8 million

There are three important points to be made about these figures. The first is that they are based on assumptions which may not prove to be realistic. If the estimates for average port utilization, or the amount that people are prepared to spend, or the cost of centre operation, or page maintenance charges turn out to be much different, then the result will be considerably altered.

The second point about the figures is that they demonstrate that the economics of a fairly large scale operation, with a quarter of a million residential users, should be such that service providers can cover their costs at prices which ordinary people may be expected to pay.

But perhaps most important is that, below about a quarter of a million residential users, service providers will be unable to cover their costs at prices appropriate for a larger scale. Either they must carry their investments over the build-up period, or charge higher prices. This explains the interest of service providers in the business market, which is less price sensitive than the residential market. It also explains the interest in services other than the provision of information for sale—such as promotional information, teleshopping and message services; and in consultancy, umbrella operations and allied services, with the purpose of generating revenue during the build-up period.

CHAPTER 4

THE MARKETPLACE

THE RESIDENTIAL MARKETPLACE

Market research

Videotex was conceived for the residential marketplace. In that sector it is a new kind of service; apart from a few isolated experiments, it has no antecedants. It has even been called a solution searching for a need: it seems a good idea, but is it wanted? Rather than launch a speculative full scale service, potential system operators have preferred to conduct market research investigations first.

The purpose of market research is to predict a general response from the behaviour of a sample. The more precisely real service conditions can be simulated, the more confidently can the general response be predicted. But precision in market research is expensive.

At one end of the scale, public demonstrations and focus group tests (group interviews with selected samples of the general public) are designed to gain a first reaction to a concept. With videotex, a large number of tests of this sort have been carried out in Europe, the USA, Canada and Japan. Generally, tests like this cannot show convincingly that an idea is a good one, but they can often show if it is a bad one. Videotex has been received favourably far more often than the reverse in this sort of test. The findings have justified more extensive, and more expensive, market research.

Full public market trials extending over a period of months lie at the other end of the market research scale. They introduce a degree of realism quite impossible with more limited tests. Videotex market trials have been planned for the early 1980s in a number of countries, including France, Holland, Switzerland, West Germany, the USA, Canada and Japan. Typically the plans involve at least a few hundred selected participants, with a heavy emphasis on the residential community. Generally they have been planned to allow plenty of time for familiarization: 6 to 12 months is typical. Some of the more important trials are described in Part 3.

To carry out a full scale public market trial effectively means a great deal of expense and effort. Inevitably some pressure can be expected from the parties involved to recoup their investments, by arranging a public service afterwards, even if only on a limited scale. This pressure was noticeable during the planning of the BPO's market trial, described in Part 2.

The Prestel market trial has gained a lot of attention because it has been the first large scale trial of its type conducted anywhere. Few results were forthcoming by the end of 1979, and those that were may not readily be transferable to other environments because of cultural, economic and other differences. Nonetheless, the results of this and other limited tests can be used as a starting point on which general predictions about videotex's appeal and limitations can be based.

The appeal of videotex

Videotex appeals because it is a single source of information in the home, which is convenient and available around the clock. It is also new and different. These are general appeals. In terms of specific services, it offers a good deal more.

It offers access to information which can be up-to-date, informative and often hard to obtain readily elsewhere—such as the price of a share, or what to do in an emergency.

It can offer a message service. Stored (mail box) messages will be important for applications like teleshopping and reservations. User-to-user messages will help reduce the frustration of busy lines and unanswered telephone calls.

It can be used for computation. It can help with calculations such as mortgage and tax routines; and with education, such as in programmed learning sequences.

And it can be used as a source of software. Some examples are for entertainment, as with programmable games; and for problem solving, for example in conjunction with a home computer.

Concerns and counter attractions

The appeals of videotex are compelling to the home user, but there are counter attractions too. The more significant ones are described here.

It requires a *change of habit*. The TV is not normally regarded as a source of information, in the same way as a reference book, for instance. Normally it is a device for passive viewing, rather than active participation. How significant the behavioural barriers might be, and how quickly people might adopt the habit of going to the TV for information, is hard to predict.

Its use will *conflict with the TV in its normal role*. Even the need for a few minutes of videotex could create a potential problem at a family's peak viewing time in a single-TV household. Multiple TVs in the household will reduce the problem; so will a dedicated videotex terminal—but at a price. The use of videotex will also conflict with the telephone; very few households have multiple telephone lines. However, the average household telephone is connected for fewer than 15 minutes per day, so there is less likelihood of conflict here than with the TV (switched on typically for several hours per day).

Its use requires *new skills*, for example in database searching. Research has shown that even the apparently simple tree-structured database is hard for some people to use. Keyword searching can be easier and more efficient, though full alphabetic keyboards (a natural, though not inevitable, consequence) are themselves somewhat inhibiting and often hard to use.

The *value of its information* will be open to question in terms of both completeness and validity. Prestel is a good example of a service which aims to provide a wide range of topics on its database to appeal to a broad population. But because of capacity limitations (numbers of pages in the hundreds of thousands to low millions) the range will remain restricted in the foreseeable future. In this respect, Prestel and systems like it are no different from other information sources like reference books. But because they may harbour an initial perception of completeness, they may lead to some disappointment later in practice.

The validity of information on videotex will also be open to question, particularly where promotional information is included, and hard to distinguish from the rest. Moreover, the medium may be perceived as lacking the authority associated with the printed word. The adequacy and intrinsic value of information on videotex will be a prime determinant of its success.

Another concern to some people is *fear of privacy invasion*. Videotex subscribers who are billed for the pages they look at will feel that 'something out there knows what I am doing'.

Some people will experience *difficulty absorbing the information* displayed. Text on TV is not easy to read, as explained in Chapter 2. The inevitable brevity of the text may be a deterrent, too, resulting from the compact editing styles which videotex encourages. Without printers or recorders, users may be deterred by what they perceive as the transience of the display.

Fear of *installation and maintenance difficulties* will be another concern. In Europe in particular, home owners are not used to having devices other than handsets attached to their telephone lines. TV servicemen and telephone engineers are generally unfamiliar with each other's territory.

To some people, these concerns and counter attractions will be serious deterrents; to others they will be insignificant. But there is little doubt about the importance which will be attached to two further considerations: price, and competing alternatives.

Price of videotex

The cost of videotex is highly volume sensitive. Its price to users will depend on its cost, and on the investment strategies of service providers (see Chapter 3). A guideline price for home users is 20 cents per minute, inclusive of TV, telephone, connect-time and page access charges. This price was already in sight for commercial services using technology available in the 1970s, at a user population around a quarter of a million.

Videotex is inexpensive compared with traditional online services, but expensive by the standards of the average consumer. Will people pay?

At the end of the 1970s, the average British family spent around 3% of net monthly income on information: books, magazines and newspapers; telephone and post; TV and radio. In other countries the proportion of net monthly income spent on information services was not very dissimilar. There was some evidence of an upward trend in real terms in those countries already enjoying a relatively high, and improving, standard of living.

The question is whether videotex will substitute for this existing expenditure, or add to it. The latter is more likely: videotex is more likely to complement, rather then replace, competing information services. If that is the case, it will presumably require a conscious decision to be made, so that a proportion of discretionary income is allocated to it rather than to something else.

Some people, with positive information needs and the necessary disposable income, will find videotex to be sufficiently valuable for them to make the allocation readily. Amongst them will be businessmen needing travel information at the touch of a button in their homes, and private investors at home needing up-to-date financial information. Others with sufficiently high income will want videotex for guidance on a choice of leisure activities. For some professionals, the provision of a terminal might be made through the company, particularly if the company is itself a videotex user. In the future such company-provided videotex terminals might become an important new perquisite like company cars.

For other people the justification for videotex will be less clear. They will be more inclined to compare videotex with alternative spending opportunities outside the information field.

Alternative spending opportunities

Rather than competing with alternative information sources, videotex will be perceived as competing with other TV-related devices. TV add-ons have become increasing widely available and sought after, and appear as certain to change the nature of TV as hi-fi did the radio. They include TV games, video-cassette recorders (VCRs), videodisc, teletext and personal computers.

Over 10 million *games* of the 'basic' dedicated chip type were sold worldwide in the last three years of the 1970s alone. Typically these games offered a few (e.g. 4–10) paddle type games like squash and tennis for two players using joysticks, retailing for around $20–$30. Other more sophisticated games have also gained popularity. At the top end of the market, they feature cartridge-loaded microprocessors offering a wide selection of games from car racing to blackjack and air/sea battles.

VCRs are for recording TV broadcasts, complete with sound, in the same way as audio tape cassettes. They allow viewers to break from dependence on fixed programme broadcasting times by 'time-shifting'—automatically recording off-air programmes for later viewing at more convenient times. A trend has been for cassette material to be pre-recorded for sale, for example popular films, opera and educational programmes.

VCR is expensive. Recording/playback devices typically cost $1000 in 1979, and three-hour blank tapes cost $30 or more. Most consumer equipment was based on one of three incompatible standards, from Philips, Sony Betamax and JVC/VHS. Even so, in 1979 around a quarter of a million units were sold in Europe, and double the number in the USA. Together with blank and pre-recorded tapes the market was worth around $1 billion.

Videodiscs permit pre-recorded material to be played back through the TV at lower prices than with VCRs. Their disadvantage is that, unlike VCRs, they cannot be used for recording broadcast programmes.

The first practical domestic videodisc system was launched by Philips/MCA (Magnavision, using the VLP format) at the end of 1978 in the USA. The disc players were priced at around $700 each, and pre-recorded 12 inch videodiscs, looking like long-playing audio records, at around $6–$20 each depending on the material, with a duration of 30 minutes on each side.

Predictions have put the value of the USA market for videodisc at $1 billion by 1982. With several major Japanese and US companies (including RCA with its Selectavision) confidently expected to join the battle for the consumer dollar before the end of 1980, this prediction may not prove to be as optimistic as it appears.

Teletext is a one-way broadcast information service offering users a selection of static pages of text and graphics. To many people it is a look-alike, low-cost alternative to videotex. From a base of around 40,000 units in Britain at the end of 1979, its popularity was growing quickly. Other countries have been conducting experiments with a view to starting similar public services in the early 1980s.

With its selection of pages limited typically to just a few hundred per channel, teletext is suitable for general information of a topical nature. As a result it is likely to command a larger residential market than videotex at first. But

55

compared with videotex it offers a less well defined commercial opportunity, its information capacity is limited, and it lacks the two-way feature of videotex which permits computation and message services. As awareness of the differences between the two services grows in the early 1980s, teletext may act as a catalyst for videotex sales.

Personal computers have achieved a rapidly growing market penetration. Well over half a million were sold in the western world in 1979, the majority in the USA. Before 1978, most personal computers were sold to home enthusiasts, but more recently they have been bought mainly by small businesses for applications such as tax accounting, payroll, inventory control, mailing lists and scientific and teaching applications. For the most part they are used off-line. Many can be plugged into a standard TV as a display device.

There is a substantial existing and growing need to supply software for these personal computers together with a source of data for them to work with. Videotex offers both possibilities. Moreover, as videotex terminals themselves gain in sophistication with full alphanumeric keyboards, processing power and additional memory to store multiple information frames and handle higher resolution graphics, they will begin to look increasingly like personal computers. The two types of terminal will begin to converge.

This is not an exhaustive list of TV-related devices aimed at the residential marketplace. Another is the projection screen for large screen viewing. All of them, however, together with videotex, will be competing for the discretionary income of the consumer.

THE BUSINESS MARKETPLACE

The appeal of videotex

Although it was conceived with the residential market in mind, videotex's initial penetration will be in the business marketplace. The reasons are clear. The need for timely, accurate information is more obvious and more urgent, and the market is less price-sensitive. Four factors will encourage videotex's use in the business marketplace:

(1) Its simplicity (no operating instructions, no training), its relatively low cost, and its use of terminals which are convivial, attractive and non-threatening.
(2) The opportunity to access different systems through a single terminal—public, closed user group and private in-house videotex services.
(3) The relative ease with which services can be implemented; not only standard terminals but complete systems for in-house operation are becoming available.

(4) The ability to provide more than one type of service on a single system—information retrieval, message services, computation and software distribution.

Probably closed user group and private in-house services will penetrate at first more rapidly than public services. Compared with public services they can offer several advantages including improved security, superior economics, custom developments and greater flexibility. Paradoxically, the impetus for private closed user group and in-house services is largely attributable to the development of public services, with their attendant publicity and large scale terminal production economies.

The business applications which are emerging for videotex are in areas where its advantages are valuable and its shortcomings are not critical.

The *information retrieval* service can be used for accessing publicly available data such as air and train timetables, government statistics, export information, business news and share price information.

Closed user group services can offer more specific business information where there is a need for some measure of security. Examples include commodity prices, share prices, seat availability for travel agents, drug information for doctors and legal records for solicitors.

In-house videotex services can provide access to information of the sort printed in newsletters, appointments, job vacancies, sales and production performance, product data and current price lists. It can also include information specific to particular groups of users in a company, such as stock information, specifications, financial control data, lists of customers and suppliers, and sales and performance targets.

Its use for *message services* will complement other electronic message systems such as telex, teletex (the proposed international super telex standard for communicating word processors), facsimile and telephone services, including recording and voice store and forward.

Videotex's appeal lies in its simplicity and potential availability, when terminals are in widespread use. Although it offers no text composition aids, and its communicating speed is relatively low, its ability to transmit messages will appeal to business users—for example, for leaving simple messages with one or more recipients when they are unobtainable on the phone. The messages could be preformatted and customized, or created specially. Typical applications could include messages about meetings, delays, schedule changes and requests for information and action. For example, in order to contact salesmen in the field a sales director could leave messages for the salesmen, already previously instructed to check the messages in the system at particular times of the day.

Another use for the message service will be in ordering goods and services from information providers—hotel and travel reservations for example.

A telex network interface would appeal to businesses without a telex terminal, or with telex terminals which are remote from message originators.

Using videotex for *computation* is similar in principle to using a remote terminal in a computer timesharing bureau service. But videotex will be less appropriate for sophisticated computations; to make the required processing power and storage available would mean jeopardizing the economics of low cost information retrieval.

Computation through videotex may find a niche between handheld and desk-top calculators, and timesharing service bureaux. Applications may include payroll, tax and accounting routines. Other applications may be designed to fit with videotex information retrieval. Thus business users might retrieve the current rates of exchange and commodity prices to perform calculations on investment returns in the commodity market.

For software distribution, videotex's virtue will be speedy delivery at relatively low cost compared with the alternative of physical distribution by tape cassette, floppy disc or plug-in solid state memory. The types of application program likely to prove appropriate for distribution through videotex will include financial routines such as taxation, purchase/sales ledger, payroll and VAT; inventory control applications such as stock recording, stock classification and replenishment control; and modelling programs.

The counter attractions

For business users, like residential users, there are counter attractions too. Using terminals based on TV technology is one. As explained in Chapter 2, the TV was not designed for displaying text. Although adequate for occasional use, adapted TVs are not really good enough to be read from over long periods. Terminals which use sharper, high resolution displays, without interlace, can be used for videotex, but are likely to be more expensive. The videotex grid, designed basically for the domestic TV, is not the same as that used by industry-standard VDUs.

Another concern centres on videotex's simplicity. This is one of its main strengths. But for many business applications requiring greater sophistication, it is also a weakness.

As videotex's advantages become more widely recognized and appreciated, it will find increasing competition from the suppliers of computer and terminal equipment interested in reaching a broader market base than in the past. With the falling cost of hardware and increasingly wide range of low cost business computers, personal computers, intelligent terminals and multifunction (word and data processing) devices, videotex will find itself facing formidable competition in the business marketplace. With all these devices, ease of learning and use will be more strongly featured than in the past.

As these trends continue, videotex itself will gain in sophistication. For example, videotex terminals will feature alphanumeric keyboards, internal processing power and storage for off-line operation. These advances will permit an extended range of functions at marginal cost. The terminals will be used to retrieve large numbers of frames into local storage for local processing, manipulation and calculation. Thus, to answer a railway timetable enquiry, an intelligent videotex terminal could provide a direct answer to a question such as the time of the first train on Saturday between towns A and B.

As a consequence of the trends described above—to a broader market base by traditional computer equipment suppliers, and to greater sophistication in videotex—the boundaries between the different business information systems will become increasingly difficult to define, and will finally disappear.

MARKET PENETRATION

Initial penetration

Business will be the lead-in marketplace for videotex, in terms of both volume of terminals sold and their usage. Both private closed user group operations and in-house services, generally among large companies keen to experiment with simple user friendly systems, will be important. The usage by businesses of publicly available videotex will attract increasing interest, often as a consequence of, rather than a precedent to, these private services.

Terminal sales and usage in the residential marketplace will follow business use. The penetration of the residential market will begin with professional people and white collar workers—not the same demographic profile as caused the growth in colour TV penetration during the late 1950s and early 1960s. The professional and business people leading off the residential market will perceive the value of videotex more readily than others, and be better positioned to judge it by results. Some will be equipped with terminals as perks. Most will already have experienced videotex in their business environments.

Usage in the residential marketplace will develop slowly and steadily as public services are introduced, and as prices drop. New users will include graduates from (more limited) teletext, and families with children for whom the educative contents of the database will be a strong incentive. Others will be those attracted to the status and prestige of the latest device.

At first, the main application in both the residential and the business marketplace will be information retrieval. Typically the information will be volatile, compact and with a high momentary value—for example, business financial information, price comparisons, classified advertisements and what to do in an emergency.

Evolution of videotex

Beyond 1983 both applications and terminal designs will begin to change. Terminals designed for the residential market will be characterized by increased intelligence and storage, permitting the local storage of multiple frames, the manipulation of stored data and the generation of alphageometric and alphaphotographic displays. The software distribution application will become important for personal computers. Message applications will also become important, including user-to-user messages which take advantage of videotex's store and forward capability. There will be a noticeable convergence between videotex terminals and personal computers.

Conceivably both videotex and personal computers will develop independently from the TV, whose prime role will continue to be entertainment, displaying video transmitted through cable, off-air, from VCRs and from videodisc. Videotex terminals and personal computers for the information role could become quite separate from the TV. In the home, such terminals could be placed in the kitchen or hall rather than in the living room, which is the centre of home entertainment. In this scenario, broadcast teletext would continue to be TV-oriented. The pressure for compatibility between teletext and videotex services would decline and even disappear.

In the business marketplace, videotex terminals will evolve, but for different reasons. Videotex will stimulate the market for low cost, simple systems. The established supplies of computer terminal and word processing equipment will respond, introducing lower priced, less sophisticated products. Videotex itself will gain in sophistication, converging with the successors of today's established terminal systems at the low end of the market. The additional cost of sophistication will be acceptable in the less price-sensitive business market.

It is possible that these evolutionary trends will result in different videotex systems being developed to meet the somewhat different needs of the residential and business markets.

Part 2

BRITAIN'S PRESTEL

the first large-scale
publicly available videotex
service

CHAPTER 5

USING PRESTEL

FINDING INFORMATION WITH PRESTEL

Information on Prestel

All four of the classes of service which videotex can provide have been demonstrated on Prestel. But during the Test Service and early public service, information retrieval was the most important. Indeed the only other service class at this time was a limited form of message, described in Chapter 7.

With the information retrieval service, users could access nearly a quarter of a million pages of information spanning a broad range of topics. Figure 5.1 shows two typical examples. One is about food prices, the other about the availability of British Airways' Stand-by seats between London and New York. Both illustrate how Prestel can be used for current (up-to-date) information.

Figure 5.1. Typical Prestel pages.

To reach the information pages they want, users need to know how to connect with Prestel, and how to search through all the pages.

Connecting with Prestel

Connecting with Prestel is simple. The procedure varies with different designs of terminal, but the following is typical. A user switches on the TV terminal and selects Prestel by pressing a button on the keypad (see Figure 5.2). Pressing another button instructs the decoder to autodial the Prestel service centre. (The decoder may also store telephone numbers for other, non-Prestel, systems.)

Through the TV loudspeaker, the user hears the telephone dialling tone, followed by the dialling pulses being generated. On some terminals the telephone number being called is displayed on the screen. The ringing tone is followed by a brief whistle indicating that the Prestel centre has answered. If the call is not answered within a set time, or if the number is busy or otherwise unobtainable, the decoder repeats the dial-up procedure using an alternative Prestel telephone number. (The decoder has two different Prestel telephone numbers stored in its memory, and starts by calling the first.)

Figure 5.2.   A typical keypad.

The decoder then carries out a short sign-on dialogue with the Prestel centre (it 'logs on') to identify itself with a 6-digit user number, and the centre checks that the terminal is authorized to access Prestel. For additional security, users can also enter a 4-digit private password number through the keypad. When the sign-on procedure has been completed, a personal 'Welcome to Prestel' page is displayed, showing the date and time of the previous connection. Figure 5.3 shows a typical welcome page.

The telephone line is now busy, just as with any normal telephone call; and the TV terminal is not available to show normal TV pictures.

The disconnection procedure ('log off') is also very simple. To end a session the user goes to page 9. Keying '9' then breaks the telephone connection. Before disconnecting, the user can inspect his Prestel bill page, which shows the charges accumulated since the last invoice and the charge for the current session. Figure 5.4 shows a typical bill page.

Searching the pages

Prestel users need to be able to find the right page from many thousands, easily and quickly. To help them do this, Prestel's pages are arranged hierarchically (the arrangement is sometimes called a *tree structure*), with every page uniquely numbered.

By keying the full page number on the keypad, a user can display a page straight away. The * and # must be keyed before and after the number; hence *N# for page N. This is fine when the full page number is known, but often it will not be, in which case users can search for a page by following indexing instructions which are displayed on the screen.

The highest level of index is at the apex of the hierarchical structure, page 0. Up to ten numbered choices (0–9) can lead off from this page to further indexing pages with more detail. In their turn they can lead on to more. To work through a hierarchy of pages leading to progressively more refined detail, a user need only select a single numbered choice at each step, keying the single corresponding digit each time on the keypad.

Figure 5.5 shows how to find 'charter flights' using high level indexes.

Index pages are called *routeing* pages. Ultimately, routeing pages lead to *end* pages. End pages contain information, rather than routeing choices. Figure 5.6 shows how an end page of information is reached. The end page in question is a railway timetable, of trains between Kings Cross and Aberdeen. In this sequence of four pages, the first three are routeing pages.

There is not always a rigid distinction between routeing and end pages. Figure 5.7 is a sequence of six pages about choosing a washing machine. The last three pages illustrate how the routeing and end information can be combined.

Figure 5.3.

Figure 5.4.

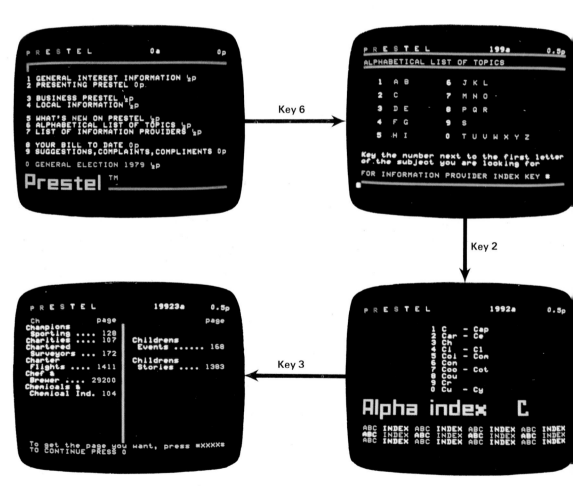

Figure 5.5.

The pages in Figure 5.7 have been supplied by *Which?*, as indicated in the top left hand corner of each (a Prestel convention). *Which?* has also set each page price, shown in the top right hand corner (also a Prestel convention). One advantage of the combined routeing/end page approach is that the price of each page can be set about the same. The alternative of free routeing pages can mean loading the prices of end pages, which users might find less acceptable.

In practice, Prestel's indexing means that there is often a number of routes to the same end page. Figure 5.8 shows three distinct routes to an end page about 'what's on' at the local cinema.

The presence of alternatives can lead to some confusion. For example, should a user seeking medical advice look under Doctors or Ailments?

Many users will find their way to Prestel end pages with the help of printed directories, which were already widely available at the start of the public service. Printed indexes show the starting page numbers of topics and information providers. Users can go straight to these pages by entering the corresponding numbers through their keypads, then make routeing choices to reach the end pages.

It is possible for users to perform a type of keyword search, where the information provider has arranged to associate letters of the alphabet with the numbers 0–9. Figure 5.9 shows such an indexing arrangement, prepared by Caxton Press for searching their encyclopaedia pages. Here the number 1 is associated with letters abc, 2 with def and so on, as shown in the schematic keypad on the second page of the sequence. To search for 'computers', a user would enter the numbers 15567 to correspond with letters COMPU. The same numbers also produce quotes on 'Compton Arthur,' 'Compton Burnett', 'Compulsory Purchase', and 'Conquistadors', as shown on the fourth page in the figure. At this point, a user can make a selection in the normal way.

Prestel's indexing can be used so that returning from an end page to an earlier point—say a high level index—is easy. Keying *o # returns to the page o index. Other uses of the * and # keys are shown in Table 5.1. They can be made sufficiently concise to etch on a keypad as a reminder.

Table 5.1. Uses of * and # keys

* #	To recall the previous frame (can be repeated up to 3 times in succession).
* *	To correct a keying error by cancelling the current keying session.
* 00	To retransmit the current frame at no charge (used if the first transmission was corrupted).
* 09	To retransmit the current page, including any updates.

Other reminders should not normally be necessary to operate Prestel. As with a telephone, just a few minutes to gain familiarity at the outset should be all that most people require.

Figure 5.6.

BECOMING A PRESTEL USER

Installation

Prestel will not be successful in the residential marketplace unless it is easy to acquire as well as easy to use. The intention is that terminals should be obtainable through regular TV distributors, and that the problems of installation and commissioning should be minimized.

Figure 5.7.

Normally, residential users of Prestel will buy or rent a terminal following a showroom demonstration. Most users will need an extension jack socket (BPO Jack 96) near where the terminal is to be installed. This can be arranged through the BPO either by the user or by the terminal distributor.

The distributor will normally inform Prestel of the impending installation for the purpose of capacity planning, and for the new subscriber's account to be opened on Prestel. The new user number (and password) can then be issued. The distributor's installation service staff can then deliver the terminal, connect it to the jack socket and (depending on the model) enter the user number and Prestel centre telephone numbers into the terminal hardware so that both can be selected by pushing a button. Acceptance testing can then be carried out by the installation engineer usually without involving any Prestel staff.

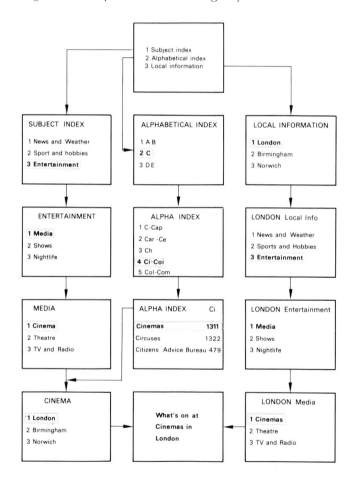

Figure 5.8. The use of different routes to an end page.

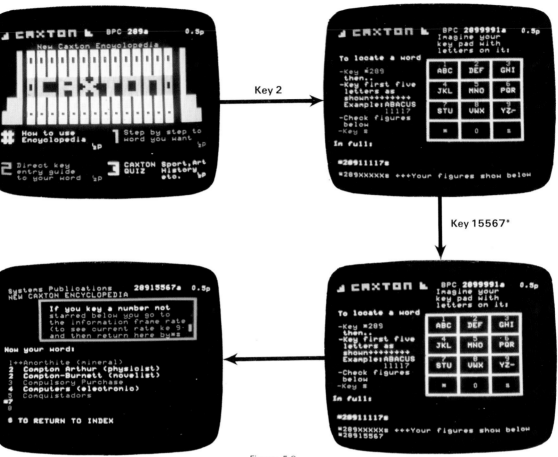

Figure 5.9.

New subscribers can expect to manage without the help of advice from a distributor thereafter, as with a normal TV, unless there are particular problems. The responsibility for terminal maintenance will rest with distributors. Because Prestel decoder components are mostly electronic (only the keypad has mechanical elements) reliability is expected to be high, and on-site maintenance should normally be a matter of interchanging circuit boards. There could, of course, be difficulties with the jack socket, which is where the BPO's responsibility begins. Inevitably, there will be some disputes over responsibility demarcations.

Billing

Each subcriber's usage statistics are recorded at the Prestel service centres.

Subscribers will be billed at quarterly intervals for their use of Prestel. The

71

telephone account will not be added; it will continue to be billed separately in the normal way. Prestel bills will show two charge categories: connect-time, and the value of priced pages accessed during the period (the tariffs are explained in Chapter 9). They may be itemized by date, but not by information provider and certainly not by page. But bills should come as no surprise to users: the charges accumulated during each session are available for scrutiny at the end of the session as already explained.

For subscribers changing their names and addresses, or discontinuing with Prestel, the procedure is much the same as with the telephone. Changing password numbers is also possible, though BPO Prestel may levy a charge for this.

CHAPTER 6

DEVELOPMENT OF PRESTEL UP TO THE EARLY PUBLIC SERVICE

ORIGINS AND EARLY TRIALS

Early development

The British Post Office's (BPO's) original aim in developing videotex was to improve the utilization of the existing voice telephone network at off-peak times. Like other telecommunications operators, it has a high investment in switching and transmission equipment to meet the peak traffic loads generated during business hours. At other times the system is relatively under-loaded. Whilst recognizing that videotex would create some additional traffic coincident with the existing peak loads, the BPO was confident that a good proportion would also be created in the evenings and at weekends.

The idea of videotex occurred to Sam Fedida while he was carrying out research work on behalf of the BPO in the early 1970s. The first system was developed on a Hewlett-Packard computer, and demonstrated in 1973. At that time the system was named 'Viewdata'. Also in the early 1970s, the BBC and IBA (The State and Independent Broadcasting Authorities, respectively) were each experimenting with teletext. Although originally the technical specifications for the BBC and IBA systems were different, agreement to the use of a common specification was reached in 1974 under the auspices of BREMA (British Radio Equipment Manufacturers Association). The representatives of the BPO's Viewdata development team agreed afterwards to share the teletext display format and a similar character set and transmission coding technique.

By 1975 the commercial potential of viewdata was becoming apparent. The BPO had discerned a need for a number of computer centres across the land to support a national public service. Following a request to tender to British industry, the BPO chose the GEC 4000 series of minicomputers as the most cost-effective solution to its computer needs. By September 1975 an experimental service using a GEC computer had been inaugurated at Martlesham Heath, the BPO's research centre.

By that time the BPO had decided on its role as Viewdata system operator, centre operator, and provider of the transmission network. As a consequence, the key roles of the terminal manufacturers and the independent information industry were clear. The need was to encourage these two disparate industries to join forces in a tripartite venture. To attract participants from these industries, and to gain insights into the nature and extent of the market, it was necessary to offer involvement in a thorough public market trial. The trial would lay the foundations for the subsequent public service.

The pilot trial

The BPO initiated a two year private pilot trial starting in January 1976. The purpose was to recruit participants from the TV and information industries, and to gain mutual experience with the system in readiness for the market trial.

In return, the BPO offered involvement in the public market trial at favourable rates with a promise of carefully analysed results, and preferential treatment in any public service thereafter.

At the start of the two year pilot trial, the BPO approached independent information providers (IPs for short) thought to have interesting applications for the residential market. Later in the pilot trial the position was reversed: the BPO was approached by IPs wanting to be involved.

It was about this time that the BPO agreed its common carrier principle. This was a significant step. It meant that the BPO would exercise no control over the information content of the database. Its role would be that of a neutral operator. So its attitude with IPs during the pilot trial was one of 'first come first served', though it did limit the number of pages allocated to each IP in order to help maintain a balanced and wide database. By the middle of 1978, over 100 IPs were contracted for the market trial.

Also during the pilot trial, the BPO demonstrated Viewdata to the TV industry, and most British TV manufacturers agreed to supply adapted TVs for the market trial. Like the IPs, the TV manufacturers were enticed by the prospects of the experience they stood to gain. The results would not be shared with non-participants, and foreign manufacturers would not be invited to join in.

In April 1978 the BPO, unable to register the name Viewdata in Britain (because it was an amalgam of two common usage words), changed the name to Prestel, whilst continuing to use viewdata as a generic term. Hence 'Prestel, the Post Office viewdata service'.

The pilot trial proceeded in a generally satisfactory way, and provided the participants with a great deal of valuable experience. As well as information retrieval, computation and message services (including a connection to telex) were successfully demonstrated.

STRATEGY FOR MASS MARKET CREATION

The BPO's calculations had convinced it that Prestel could be offered at prices which would be low enough to attract the mass market. But to do this required the economies of scale of a mass volume operation. Its strategy was to reach that stage as quickly as possible.

It meant investing heavily in computer centres across the nation to bring Prestel within the local call area of most people. From the start, the computer centres would offer databases with a wide selection of information—something for everyone. TV terminals would also have to be widely available in the showrooms to catch the attention of the general public.

To help the TV industry, the BPO overturned its earlier policy controlling the connection of terminal devices to the telephone network. In 1977 it agreed to permit the use of integral modems in Prestel TV terminals. Following general approval by the BPO of individual terminal designs, the TV industry would be free to connect Prestel terminals to the telephone network without the direct involvement of the BPO. Later, this relaxation in control was extended to apply to any terminal capable of receiving Prestel with or without a TV tuner.

But as the pilot trial proceeded, many of the IPs and TV industry participants continued to harbour doubts about the potential of the residential market. Moreover, their investments were exceeding expectations. The unexpectedly slow take-off of teletext had led to doubts about the saleability of screened information in the home. The semiconductor suppliers wanted large orders to launch their LSI chip sets, but the TV manufacturers were reluctant to place the orders until assured of the market potential.

Both the IPs and the TV manufacturers wanted a commitment from the BPO to a public service after the market trial, even if only on a limited basis. What was needed was an assured market. It seemed obvious that this was the business market, which was in any case already showing strong interest.

Consequently the BPO began to encourage IPs with business applications, and TV manufacturers to develop special purpose business terminals. A danger of the switch in emphasis was that it ran counter to the original intention of encouraging the use of the telephone at off-peak times. But it was seen as a means to an end—that end being the residential market, which ultimately would dominate.

To help encourage its partners, and in recognition of the likely shortcomings of the market trial itself, the BPO announced in February 1978 that the public service would start anyway in the first quarter of 1979, and that the market trial would be re-named the Test Service. The reaction from the IPs and the TV industry to the announcement was mixed. On the one hand they were encouraged, and on the other rather concerned about the early date, which would mean entering a public service without the benefit of full market trial results, and with insufficient time fully to develop their services.

So the BPO's strategy changed its shape during Prestel's gestation. It evolved into one of rapid acceleration of both business and residential markets independent of the outcome of a public market trial. The capital authorized by the BPO (about $50 million inclusive, to about the end of 1980) was planned for spending primarily on computer centres and software to support a large scale service, rather than alternatives such as the production of decoder chips or external adaptors.

Moreover it was not part of the BPO's strategy to attempt to target specific market sectors within the general residential and business communities. That would have run counter to its role as a neutral common carrier, and could be better undertaken by the IPs and the TV industry.

THE TEST SERVICE

The Test Service plans: aims, sample selection and monitoring

The original market trial was renamed the Test Service following the commitment to a public service which was announced in February 1978. But the aims remained the same. The prime aim was to predict the size and nature of the market in the period up to 1985. Other key aims were concerned with the types of information to be offered, pricing policies, terminal design, database maintenance, computer operation, billing arrangements, and legal and copyright issues.

The number of participants planned for the Test Service was 1550, equal to the number of terminals promised from the suppliers. Of the 1550, 850 would be residential participants, and 700 would be business participants. Each participant would be involved for a period of six months, though because of delays in obtaining and commissioning terminals, the Test Service was expected to run for a total of twelve months. The first users were to be connected in the summer of

1978 and the last by the year end, so that the Test Service would be over by the summer of 1979.

Participants were to be selected in three geographical areas: London, Birmingham and Norwich. The residential sample was not expected to be representative of the population as a whole, but rather to provide data about the socio-economic classes constituting the target Prestel market.

The Test Service participants were to be charged at rates representative of the later public service, e.g. TV terminals would be made available to residential users at a premium rental of about 50% following a free introductory period.

The participants were to be monitored continuously using face-to-face interviews, and by the automatic collection of usage statistics at the Prestel Test Service centre. The interviews were to be carried out in three phases: before terminal delivery, two months following terminal delivery, and at the end of the six months period.

In contrast with the pilot trial, the services available through the system were to be reduced to information retrieval, together with a limited message service permitting users to respond to IPs through a 'response frame' facility. The purpose of this service reduction was to ensure simplicity, and to preserve the computer's response time for the all-important information retrieval service.

Test Service conduct and results

In practice, the Test Service fell somewhat short of the plan described above. It started late, in September 1978, and was not expected to finish until well into 1980.

The delayed start was due to software difficulties, and to a continuing shortage of terminals. Consequently the build-up in number of participants was much slower than expected. Fewer than half the terminals scheduled for delivery by the end of 1978 were in place by the middle of 1979. Moreover, the software for automatically monitoring usage at the Prestel centre was still not working by the end of 1979.

As if this were not enough, IPs were unable to fill and maintain the expected 180,000 test pages, largely because of a shortage of editing terminals and editing time. The difficulties were accelerated when the public service began operating in parallel, causing further confusion.

The initial achieved sample of Test Service users fell well short of the 1550. The figure was 902: 378 residential and 524 business. But a decision to extend the Test Service from a one-year to a two-year activity, with users participating for twelve consecutive months rather than six, permitted the sample to be increased to around the number originally planned.

The residential sample was biased towards the 'AB' socio-economic class (managerial and professional classes, and white collar workers), and generally to high information users. The business sample included public and private companies, together with nationalized industries, educational establishments, local government, partnerships and other industry sectors.

By the end of 1979, an analysis of the early Test Service results indicated clearly that the business participants were responding more enthusiastically to Prestel than the residential participants. More of the latter seemed likely to reject Prestel at the end of the trial than to keep it, though the reverse was true with the business sample.

ROLES OF THE PARTICIPANTS

BPO Prestel

Prestel involves the participation and co-operation of three disparate industries: the BPO, the IPs and the TV and equipment industry.

The BPO has several key responsibilities with Prestel. As centre operator, it is responsible for the operation of the computer centres. This includes software development, hardware selection, testing, site selection, installation, operation and security. As carrier, the BPO is responsible for transmission network arrangements, service centre interconnection, and the availability of exchange and subscriber lines.

BPO Prestel is also responsible for its share of promotional activities, and for subscriber connection, accounting and billing. The subscribers will certainly regard BPO Prestel—rightly or wrongly—as the full provider of the service.

Although its relationship with the other parties is supposedly on equal partner terms, the reality is that it is the leader and key decision maker.

The BPO Prestel operation is established on the basis of an independent profit centre, though still within Post Office Telecommunications—a position which it has described as the nearest it can get to a wholly-owned subsidiary. BPO Prestel aims to contribute to the profitability of Post Office Telecommunications in its own right, even though the extra telephone revenues arising from Prestel will not be credited to the Prestel profit centre. The main reason for this is to avoid possible criticism of unfair advantage. Other organizations wishing to compete—and the BPO has not discouraged such a possibility—could legitimately complain if the public monopoly BPO were cross-subsidizing a part of its own operation, thereby assisting it to compete unfairly.

Role of the IPs

The IPs are responsible for preparing and maintaining their information on the Prestel database. Their aim is to enhance their business interests through profit and revenue growth. Like BPO Prestel, they are primarily interested in terminal *usage*.

In line with the strategy of BPO Prestel, the IPs have produced pages of information which cover a broad range of subjects, to 'provide something for everyone'. Because of capacity limitations, however, BPO Prestel has had to restrict the number of IPs in the early public service, though it plans to lift this restriction later on as more capacity becomes available.

As a result of its neutral status, BPO Prestel has permitted IPs to join the service on a 'first come first served' basis. Its attitude has been that market forces will ensure that only the better IPs will continue with the system. For commercial reasons, BPO Prestel might in future be tempted to favour certain IPs having what it regards as more appropriate applications. At the same time it will want to maintain at least a semblance of impartiality if it is to continue to preserve its position of neutrality. Meanwhile, the leading IPs have taken advantage of their experience with and knowledge of the system. Many have offered their services as *umbrella IPs*, sub-letting portions of their own databases to *sub-IPs*. They have also generated additional revenue through consulting activities of all sorts.

To represent their interests as a group, the IPs formed their own trade association called AVIP (Association of Viewdata Information Providers) at the start of 1978. AVIP is a self-financing body, paid for through IP subscriptions. Just one year after its formation almost 100 IPs (about 60% of the total at that time) had become members.

Virtually all the Test Service IPs opted to join in the public service. They signified this through letters of intent to BPO Prestel, though they had yet to sign public service contracts at the end of 1979.

Role of the TV and equipment industry

The role of the TV and equipment industry is to supply and service adapted TV terminals, purpose-designed terminals and ancillary equipment for Prestel.

The main interest of the established TV manufacturers has been in the prospective mass residential market. Its aim is to sell TV terminals; their usage is important, but only as a means to an end. But the original excitement which Prestel caused has been coloured somewhat by a realization of the potential of alternative new investment opportunities, and concern about the rate of emergence of the residential marketplace (see Chapter 3).

The success of Prestel depends on the combined efforts of these three separate industries: the BPO, the IPs and the TV and equipment industry. They are three somewhat unlikely bedfellows, without much previous experience of mutual co-operation. Yet if one were to fail, Prestel—at least as initially conceived—would fail too.

To co-ordinate activities between the three has entailed the establishment of a hierarchy of planning and decision making groups. The main forum for Prestel discussion is the Prestel Liaison Group (PLG). There are also a number of sub-groups to co-ordinate activities at a more detailed level.

That the structure and the will for co-operation exists between the three service providers reflects great credit on the people involved, and has been a major contributor to the speed with which Prestel services have been implemented.

START OF THE PUBLIC SERVICE

Opening Prestel centres

To demonstrate its determination to stick to the announced schedule, BPO Prestel began a public service in February 1979. But it was only a limited public service run from the Test Service centre in London's Gresham Street, and it was restricted to residential users in the London area. The restriction was caused by continuing delays in software and in TV terminal delivery—the same delays which had affected the Test Service.

The real start of the public service began some six months later in September 1979, following the opening of dedicated service centres in London. The two centres to open first were at Fleet (called 'Byron') and Wood Green (called 'Juniper'). Both held identical, replicated databases. They were copied from a master database held at a third computer centre—called an update centre—at Clerkenwell ('Duke').

Shortly afterwards in December, a further service centre was opened in Birmingham ('Dickens'). Further service centres were to be opened in the early months of 1980 at Ealing and Eltham in London, and in other major cities outside London. These plans are described in Chapter 10.

By the end of 1979 around 2000 users in total (including Test Service users and IPs) were connected to the service centres, and over 10 million page accesses had been recorded since the beginning of the Test Service. More than 130 IPs had completed over 160,000 pages of information on a wide range of subjects on the system. But compared with the original plans, the start of the public service was somewhat muted. The rapid growth to mass market volumes was inevitably going to take longer than expected, to give time for the service to be improved and for TV terminals to become more generally available.

CHAPTER 7

PRESTEL'S INFORMATION RETRIEVAL SERVICE

STRUCTURE OF THE DATABASE

Arrangement of pages

Prestel's pages can be imagined to be arranged in the form of a pyramid. The index page at the top (page 0) has ten choices (0 to 9) each leading to ten pages at the level below, and so on down to the lowest, tenth, level. This is a useful concept, but it is somewhat misleading. Actually, the database structure is more flexible than the simple pyramid tree structure implies for several reasons.

A *Prestel page* is the smallest item of information which a user can address directly. But each page can be extended over up to 26 additional display screenfuls, each called a frame. A frame is identified by its parent page number, plus a following alphabetic character a,b,c,...,z. Frames can only be reached via their parent pages. To get to the last frame of several behind a parent page means going through all of them in turn. Prestel has no jump or reverse procedures for finding frames.

Frames permit a logical topic to be extended over more than the capacity of a single screenful without the designer having to use other *filials*. Figure 7.1 shows several frames following page number 10332. Page 10332 is a filial of its parent page 1033. So are the other pages, numbered 10330–10334, on either side of it, i.e. on the same level.

Not all the pages or frames theoretically available need to be used in a practical Prestel database. Indeed with a theoretical capacity of more than 10^{10} screenfuls, that would be quite impractical. Users keying a valid page number which does not exist as an entity on the database are informed through a system message appearing at the foot of the current display.

There is another reason why Prestel's database structure is more flexible than the conceptual pyramid implies. This is because numbered routeing choices on a parent page do not have to lead to corresponding filial pages. Rather, such choices can lead to pages in quite different locations in the database, as shown in Figure 7.2.

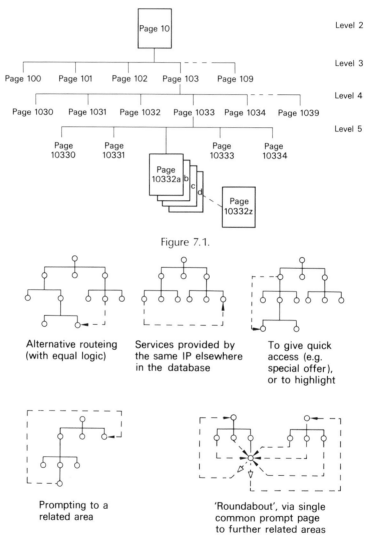

Figure 7.1.

Alternative routeing (with equal logic)

Services provided by the same IP elsewhere in the database

To give quick access (e.g. special offer), or to highlight

Prompting to a related area

'Roundabout', via single common prompt page to further related areas

Figure 7.2.

This arrangement brings many advantages. One is that designers can arrange for users to jump to new areas of the database by selecting a single choice. They can cross-reference from one area to another. For example, a user might be in a part of the database concerned with do-it-yourself. By keying a single digit, he can jump to another part of the database for information about paint stocks and prices.

The correct term to describe the Prestel database structure is not tree structure, but *relational net,*, emphasizing how it can be conceived as a network of interlinking pages according to the designer's purpose.

Database capacity

The actual database capacity is restricted by the physical capacity of the disc storage units attached to the computers at the service centres. At the start of the public service, the disc capacity was 250 megabytes, equivalent to about 250,000 pages (see Chapter 8). Each page (and frame) of information was recorded on the disc file in a fixed length record of about 1000 bytes (960 characters for the 40 × 24 display, plus a fixed overhead).

Not all of this capacity was available for public information pages. Some was allocated to system operating overheads, and some to closed user groups, leaving about 180,000 pages for public use. BPO Prestel's plan has been to expand the page capacity in two ways: first by fitting higher capacity, high performance disc units, and later by replacing the replicated database with a distributed database arrangement. Following this later change, the overall page capacity of the network will no longer be equivalent to the capacity of one of the databases. Rather, it will begin to move towards the sum of the capacities of all the individual databases, as explained in Chapter 8.

CONTENT OF THE DATABASE

IPs' databases

To help make it attractive, Prestel offers a wide range of topics from antiques to washing machines, and from book reviews to job vacancies. The breadth is ensured through the involvement of a large number of independent IPs. There were over 130 registered with BPO Prestel at the start of the public service.

Each registered IP rents part of the capacity of the database from BPO Prestel. BPO Prestel itself fills the pages at the top two levels, plus several hundred more at lower levels. These pages are used for a variety of reasons. One is for high level indexing by subject and by IP. Another is for news about Prestel itself—its progress and problems, together with some predictions for the future. A third is for advice and comments for both users and IPs.

IPs' portions of the Prestel database (called 'IP databases') can start at level 3. Each IP in this position has a 3-digit entry page number allocated by BPO Prestel. Other IPs' entry pages start at lower levels. Each IP's database can be visualized as a smaller version of the overall pyramid, with the IP the custodian of all the page numbers below his entry point, i.e. preceded by his own 3-digit number. But in practice, each IP is restricted to an allocated number of pages according to his rental agreement with BPO Prestel. At the start of the public service this number lay between 100 and 10,000, in blocks of 100. Even 10,000 is only a tiny fraction of the theoretical number of addressable pages below level 3.

With 999 3-digit numbers in total, and many fewer IPs, there are plenty of spares. Some IPs have chosen to take more than one 3-digit number. IPs themselves can sub-let part of their own database space allocation to sub-IPs. (Indeed BPO Prestel encouraged them to do this during the Test Service.) IPs sub-letting are called 'umbrella organizations'.

Cross-referencing permits IPs to design their routeings so that users can jump around within their own databases, or across to other IPs' databases. The latter clearly requires co-operation between the IPs in question, not only in terms of design, but also editing and payment.

IPs and subjects

At the start of the Prestel public service, about 130 IPs at level 3 and more than 50 other sub-IPs shared the capacity of around 180,000 pages. The average allocation per IP was about 1000 pages with bottom and top limits of 100 and 10,000 respectively. Very roughly one-third of all the pages were aimed at the residential marketplace, one-third at the business marketplace and one-third at both.

The IPs varied from small private businesses employing no more than a handful of staff (in principle, individuals can be IPs) to giant corporations in the public as well as the private sector.

Table 7.1 shows some of the major industry sectors represented, together with examples of the IPs in each sector. Table 7.2 is an extraction from the list of subjects as it stood during part of 1979. Both tables illustrate the wide scope of the database. They also serve to illustrate its limitations, resulting from the restricted capacity.

IPs' database design

Although in principle IPs are free to design their databases more or less how they want, in practice the constraints are considerable. They are in terms of factors such as display size, colours, typography and overall conventions. Nonetheless,

IPs have learned quickly how effective design can encourage viewing.

There are two, related, aspects to the subject: database structure and individual page design.

Table 7.1. Example industry sectors represented by Prestel IPs

Travel	ABC, Thomas Cook, Cosmos Holidays, British Airways, British Tourist Authority, British Rail.
Banking and Finance	American Express, Datastream, Stock Exchange.
Education	Open University, Health Education Council, British Library.
Leisure	Sportsdata, Grand Metropolitan.
Government	Department of Industry.
Publishing	Link House, Eastel, IPC.
Retailing and Marketing	Debenhams, Great Universal Mail Order, Comet.
Consultancy Services	Butler Cox and Partners.
Consumer Advice	Consumers' Association.

Table 7.2. Example topics from under letter 'c'

Calculators
Calories
Cameras
Camping
Cancer Research
Capital Gains Tax
Car Accessories
Car Buying Guide
Car Ferries
Car Insurance
Car Racing
Caravans
Careers
Castles
Catering
Central Film Library
Central Office of Information
Central Statistical Office
Champions
Charities
Chartered Surveyors
Chemicals
Childrens Events
Childrens Stories
Cinemas, etc. ...

With *database structure*, the need is to match the logical flow of pages—routeing and end pages—to the perception of the user. This may sound easy, but experience shows it often is not. What is logical to a designer may not be logical to a user.

The designer is confronted by a number of choices of how to arrange the pages. The pages do not have to follow a tree structure, as many IPs at the start of the public service were discovering.

The choice of database architecture is influenced by the nature of the information to be structured. Advice on choosing a holiday resort can lead to an approach quite different from information about, say, parliamentary procedures.

Page design is largely dictated by the small amount of display space available. Not all the 960 characters of Prestel's grid are available for use in practice. Both the top and bottom character rows are reserved for page headings and system messages respectively. The first character position in each row is taken by a control character unless the following characters use the basic character set, in white (see Chapter 2). But because dense text looks daunting on the screen and is hard to read, and because of the need for captions, the practical page capacity is about 100 words.

Table 7.3. IPs' experience with database structure

Indexing to the entry point (mainly in the first two levels) must be clear and concise.

The entry point welcome page must be clearly distinguishable, yet must transmit useful information too.

Routeing to end pages must be quick, entailing the minimum number of intervening levels.

Using the cross-referencing facility can greatly enhance the database structure.

Menu choices must be clear and complete.

As well as menu choices, routeing pages should deliver information where possible, to sell on.

Table 7.4. IPs' experience with page design

Text density should be limited (e.g. to 100 words maximum for a 'full' page).

Symbols (like %) are better than words.

Unnecessary punctuation should be avoided (USA, not U.S.A.).

Choices must be unambiguous, complete and exclusive.

Information should be centred—the curved screen encourages a central focal point.

Colour changes or indents are preferable to line breaks for paragraph changes.

The number of colours on a page should be restricted to three at the most.

Colours should be used effectively; the clarity sequence is white, yellow, cyan, green, magenta, red, blue.

The information imparted in this restricted area must stand on its own, and also link with its neighbouring pages. The message should be clear and concise, and also consistent. To achieve these aims requires careful attention to a number of matters including the wording of captions and text, punctuation, spacing, use of colours and graphics and overall page layout.

Experience has given the IPs a number of valuable insights into the basics of database structure and individual page design. Existing material cannot simply be copied on to Prestel. The points in Tables 7.3 and 7.4 summarize some of the more important lessons.

Database maintenance procedure

The aim of database maintenance (*editing*) is to permit IPs to change their database structures and page contents easily, conveniently, and at low cost, to encourage them to keep their data relevant and up-to-date. IPs' changes must conform to BPO Prestel's specifications for data layout, and type of change. Five types of change are permissible:

enter, which permits the creation of new pages (or frames) subject to certain constraints

delete, which permits the deletion of a page (or frame) subject to certain constraints

amend, which permits the alteration of a page (or frame) but not its choice selections

overwrite, which permits the alterations of both content and choice of selections

copy, which permits the copying of a page (or frame) to another part of the database.

IPs enter their changes remotely. At the time of the early public service they could do this in two ways: by editing online using a standard BPO Prestel Mark 1 editing terminal, or by transferring changes from another computer either offline or online to the Prestel computer.

Editing online with a standard Mark 1 editing terminal was the more widely used alternative at the start of the Test Service.

Mark 1 editing terminals consist of a full alphanumeric keyboard, with colour and graphics entry keys, attached to a standard Prestel colour terminal. Designed by BPO Prestel as a temporary expedient, the Mark 1 editing terminal has been relatively cheap to rent, but slow to use. It has no provision for local information storage, or intelligence to assist with text creation. Transmission speeds are 1200/75 bits per second to and from the Prestel computer respectively, the same as with a regular user terminal.

Because it can only work online, the terminal ties up a port during editing, and can lead to expensive telephone bills (though BPO Prestel's charge to IPs for editing telephone connection was initially at local call rates). IPs have found that the time for an experienced operator to enter relatively simple text-only pages under favourable conditions can average around 5 minutes. More complex pages with coloured graphic designs can take much longer—even one or two hours.

87

Figure 7.3 shows a Mark 1 editing terminal.

Transferring changes prepared offline could be done in two ways at the start of the public service: batch update by magnetic tape, and online update from another computer.

Figure 7.3. Mark 1 editing terminal.

At the start of the Test Service, a handful of IPs were using magnetic tape to update their database. Some already held the information in their own computers for other purposes, and had developed their own software to produce the tapes. Others were using the Preview package developed by Langton Information Systems, providing a range of features for converting file records to the appropriate Prestel format.

Bulk update online from another computer was restricted to just one user at the start of the public service, the Stock Exchange. Only one bulk update port was available, at the relatively slow speed of 300 bits per second. BPO Prestel was planning to extend the bulk update facility during 1980, by introducing more asynchronous bulk update ports at update centres.

As from 1980, Mark 2 editing terminals were expected to be available to permit IPs to prepare their changes offline and to enter them through the bulk update ports. Several designs of Mark 2 editing terminals had been developed and demonstrated by private industry during 1979, though none of them were in regular use.

RESPONSE FRAMES

Purpose of response frames

With a *response frame* (a Prestel term) a user can send a message back to an IP through Prestel. For this to happen, the IP must have prepared a response frame in the first place which the user can find his way to. And the IP must have made clear on the frame how it is to be completed and 'returned' by the user, and what the consequences are.

Response frames are a message service, not an information retrieval service. But they are discussed in this chapter because they are closely allied to information pages. They permit users to respond to information shown by IPs, for example to order items for delivery usually through the mail in the normal way.

Over a dozen IPs were offering response frames at the start of the public service, on topics such as book clubs (e.g. membership) and travel (e.g. brochures). Response frames permit users to place orders on the spot when their interest is at its highest—the moment it has been whetted.

Items ordered can be free of charge or paid for on or after delivery. An alternative is for IPs to offer credit card purchasing at the time the response frame is completed. Here, a purchaser can enter his credit card number through the keypad. On receipt of the card number, the IP can arrange to complete the transaction through the purchaser's credit card company in the normal way.

The lack of a signature accompanying the credit card number introduces an additional element of risk, but one which is already widely accepted as with telephone credit card ordering.

Procedure for using response frames

The response frame transaction is initiated by a user retrieving an IP's response frame which invites him to release details of his name and address to the IP.

The first frame in Figure 7.4 shows an offer of fuchsia plants made by *She* magazine. The offer is for an order form. The user first keys **#** as instructed on the frame. The response frame is then displayed again, complete with the user's name; address and telephone number (taken from the user's details which are stored at the service centre). The second frame in the figure is complete with user's name, address and telephone number.

The user then has the option of sending the response frame by keying 1, or cancelling by keying 2. On keying 1, the service centre computer transfers the frame as displayed on the user's screen to a message pool in the database. When the IP next connects to Prestel his welcome page informs him that a new message is waiting. The IP must then access a specific page number to retrieve the message (identical to the one sent by the user) for display on his own screen.

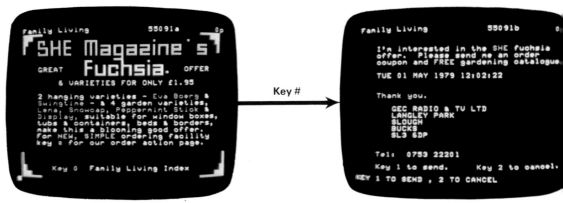

Figure 7.4. Response frames.

At the start of the public service, IPs could remove one message at a time from the pool for display, but could not store or return it. BPO Prestel's expectation then was to introduce an improved facility, as explained in Chapter 9.

Figure 7.5 is a schematic of the response frame procedure.

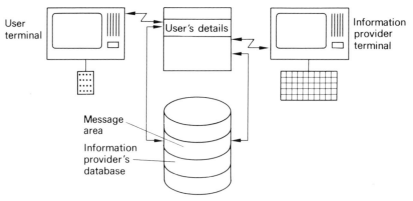

Figure 7.5. Schematic of the response frame.

An extension of this simple procedure permits a user to enter numeric information on to the response frame by using his keypad. Here, the IP sets up a number of blank entries to be filled in by the user, for example to specify the catalogue or reference numbers of goods, together with quantities required. The user terminates each entry by keying #, which moves the cursor to the start of the next entry point. Mistakes can be corrected by keying ** to reposition the cursor.

PUBLISHING ON PRESTEL
Editing control and liability

One problem which is immediately apparent from the range of public and private information on the database is the question of editorial control over the nature, volume and balance of pages on the system.

BPO Prestel's policy has been to avoid becoming entangled with this issue, and to adopt instead a neutral common carrier role. Its reluctance to get involved has been based on sensitivity to '1984' criticism, the fear that competition amongst IPs might be stifled, and the sheer practical difficulty of vetting the number of frames involved. In any case there are of course legal constraints on publishing, such as the Trade Descriptions Act, libel and obscenity laws. BPO Prestel has an indemnifying clause in its contracts with IPs to cover it against civil liability, but is vulnerable in cases of a criminal nature against which it cannot be indemnified.

But despite its reluctance over editorial control, it has had to get involved. It has had to limit the space available to individual IPs to help ensure a large number of them, and hence a wide information coverage. And it has barred information it considers to be grossly unsuitable or offensive, though still legal.

Conflicting pressures will be brought to bear on the BPO over its open policy on editorial control. On the one hand the experience of both the press and broadcasters is that pressures—political, legal, industrial and so on—are inevitable and often irresistible. There is bound to be legislation to control Prestel's information content in some form. But on the other hand there may be equal pressures, for example from consumer-oriented bodies like the Office of Fair Trading and the Department of Consumer Protection and Prices Control, to maintain an open database with free access to an essentially public facility. These bodies might be reluctant to see control passed from BPO Prestel to umbrella organizations, themselves able to dictate entry conditions and prices, and perhaps with the potential for a price fixing cartel, without the same level of scrutiny which BPO Prestel as a public corporation has to endure.

Under its public service contracts with IPs, BPO Prestel aims to protect itself as best it can from actions brought against it in its role as carrier from the possible consequences of information presented to users by IPs. Basically the contract provides protection against criminal liability, civil liability and 'offensive bad taste' actions.

The whole question of editorial control over a new medium like Prestel raises fundamental issues like sovereignty over the information handling process, ownership of information, definition of publishing and publisher, freedom of information, information disclosure in the public interest, privacy, copyright protection, and many related concepts.

It is likely that a new legal and social framework, perhaps similar to that appearing for computers themselves, will emerge as a result of the spread of

Prestel, related to the substantially increased access to information by the public which it can provide. In this process the BPO may find itself an unwilling pioneer.

IPs' code of practice

The IPs have recognized the need not only to safeguard their own information from the standpoint of legality and acceptability, but also to ensure its quality as a whole. The code of practice produced by AVIP, the Association of Viewdata IPs (see Chapter 6) is an attempt to document the guidelines for IPs' good practice on information presentation and advertising.

Table 7.5.   IPs' code of practice: quality and pricing recommendations

The name of the organization or individual providing information should be clearly and unambiguously stated on each Prestel page.

Where information is of a topical nature it should be clearly dated and if necessary timed.

Distinctions between information and advertising should be clearly drawn.

Invalid routes should be avoided.

The information to be found on the next page or pages should be clearly if briefly stated on the given page.

Users should under no circumstances be misled about the information resulting from a page choice.

Price changes should be clearly and unambiguously stated on a given page.

Changes of information provider should be clearly and unambiguously stated on a given page.

The use of double digit keying is prohibited unless the full cost implications are explained to the user.

IPs must provide the route that is most economical to the user.

The price of each page of information must be clearly stated.

Users must be in no doubt as to the consequence of using the response page facility.

IPs should keep documented records of all the information they provide on Prestel.

Unauthorized changes by IPs or sub-contractors to other IPs or sub-contractors' pages is strictly prohibited.

Table 7.6.   IPs' code of practice: advertising principles

The general principle governing Prestel advertising is that it should be legal, decent, honest and truthful.

An advertisement must be clearly distinguishable as such (e.g. by labelling 'advertisement').

All descriptions, claims and comparisons should be capable of substantiation.

Advertisements must comply with the provisions of the Trade Descriptions Act, 1968, in all respects.

Advertisements indicating price comparisons or reductions must comply with the Trade Descriptions Act, 1968.

Orders placed through Prestel for advertised goods and services constitute a contract.

Some of the more important quality and pricing recommendations are summarized in Table 7.5. Advertising principles are summarized in Table 7.6.

Security and copyright

IPs are naturally concerned about the security of their data, both from other IPs who might corrupt it or copy it, and from users who might want to copy it to reduce their access needs, and hence costs.

Each IP is only able to enter his own section of the database for editing, using a unique password number to do so. The Prestel software checks to ensure that each IP only edits pages within his allocated range.

The issue of copyright is a complex one, and one which was still not clear at the start of the public service. It has been a cause of concern to IPs since the start of their involvement with Prestel. There appear to be two basic premises. First, putting existing copyright material on to Prestel requires the permission of the copyright owner. Second, material which is created or arranged for Prestel constitutes an original work protected by copyright.

Because of its position as a neutral carrier BPO Prestel does not plan to seek any assignment of copyright on material put on to Prestel. Consequently IPs must take responsibility for the copyright implications of their material. If they are not the copyright owner, they need to ensure that they have the copyright owner's permission to store material on Prestel, as well as for all the uses to which it might be put. IPs also need to ensure that, if they are the copyright owner, their material is used only in ways for which they have given permission.

In 1977 the British Copyright Council indicated that copyright owners had the right to control the uses of their work on Prestel in terms of publishing, broadcasting and performing in public. However, merely by entering their pages on to Prestel, IPs might be seen to be giving permission for their information to be used in some of these ways—though precisely what permission is unclear. Nonetheless IPs should be aware of this, and should consider what permission they might be giving to BPO Prestel. They should also consider what right they are giving to users who pay to look at pages according to the prices asked.

Of course individual IPs will have different viewpoints about these questions, depending on their type of information. Advertising material will presumably benefit from the maximum possible exposure, so IPs will want to give blanket permission for its wide usage, free of charge. On the other hand, IPs selling information will usually want to retain control over their pages.

Clearly some of the ways of using information on Prestel are essential to its success, and few IPs would want to restrict them. Others may be ones which IPs want to control themselves. For IPs to enforce control will require both the detection of copyright infringements, and sanctions against infringements. Certainly, infringements are likely to be encouraged by the lack of any licensing arrangement on the part of IPs.

CHAPTER 8

PRESTEL SYSTEM COMPONENTS

SYSTEM ARCHITECTURE

Prestel service centres will be distributed across Britain to be within local call telephone reach of the majority of the population. An analysis which the BPO carried out in the mid-1970s showed that, for simple information retrieval, the performance of the disc and central storage of the service centre computers were likely to be critical. The analysis showed that computers with around 200–400 ports were likely to be about the right size—a decision which the BPO has remained confident about since.

Service centres which can be reached with a local telephone call help to reduce telephone charges and keep access paths short, so that inexpensive short haul modems can be used. BPO Prestel's intention has been to limit the amount of 'out of area' access to each Prestel service centre, though there will be some STD* ports.

BPO Prestel's intention has been to open service centres in densely populated areas at first in anticipation of demand, as explained in Chapter 10.

For the early years of the public service, the plan has been for identical replicated databases to be held at each service centre. The information pages would be maintained at one or more central update centres, and changes transmitted to these service centres to keep all the databases in line. At the start of the public service, BPO Prestel was hopeful that one update centre would support around 15 service centres. In practice this may prove somewhat optimistic. The

* Subscriber trunk dialling, the BPO's term for dial-yourself long distance connection.

target was for a maximum interval of 30 minutes between IPs' changes recorded on the update centre database to be transmitted to the service centres.

At the start of the public service, the transmission links connecting update centres with the service centres were rated at 2400 bits per second. The plan was for these to be replaced with high capacity 9600 bits per second trunk lines using X 25-like protocols. These lines were to be designed for two-way transmission to permit statistics, response frames and other data to be transmitted back to the update centre.

Later in the public service, the plan was for the replicated database arrangement to be superseded by a network of distributed databases each containing a mix of local as well as common data, as explained in Chapter 10.

SERVICE CENTRES AND COMPUTERS

Prestel service centres will be located in places like telephone exchanges. They will be designed for minimum floorspace, no air conditioning, and only a limited support staff to keep costs down. Ultimately, unmanned operation is envisaged.

The computers need to be rugged and reliable for continuous, 24 hour operation. They also need to be inexpensive, with a good input/output performance. A further stipulation made by the BPO at the time of its selection exercise in 1975 was that the computers should be British.

The BPO chose the GEC 4000 series of computers following its invitation to British industry to tender. The series is well established for real-time applications such as in laboratories, industrial plants and traffic control. Its design is unusual, particularly the arrangements for hardware message handling and task scheduling. But it seems to be well suited for Prestel.

The 4000 series ordered for the early public service can take six input/output channels: one basic multiplexor for local peripherals such as printer and archiving magnetic tape, and up to five external multiplexors. Because of addressing constraints, each external multiplexor is limited to a maximum of 96 lines in the Prestel configuration.

BPO Prestel chose to configure its computers initially with four 70 megabyte discs on one of the external multiplexors, and a total of just 208 lines on the other four, although it expected to increase this number to a maximum of 384 later.

Four 70 megabyte discs can hold 250,000 frames at 1 kilobyte per frame. Simulations carried out on a GEC 4000 series computer with just one small 9.6 megabyte disc showed that requests arriving at an average rate of 30 per second could be handled within 2 seconds on 99% of occasions. Predictions based on this have indicated that a single 70 megabyte disc could provide the same performance for a request arrival rate of 40 per second.

Is 40 arrivals per second enough? BPO Prestel's fairly cautious assumption has been that the average user once connected to a service centre will request a new page every 10 seconds (this includes both disc access and transmission time). At 10 seconds per page, the 70 megabyte discs should be able to support 400 users at 40 requests per second. So on this score, the computer should be able to handle 208 user lines all connected simultaneously.

Higher capacity 270 megabyte discs are available for the GEC 4000 series computers. Four of these could be attached to each external multiplexor, giving a four-fold increase in storage capacity to around 1 million information pages. Probably these would have little effect on service performance. But BPO Prestel has planned to raise the storage capacity on each service centre in phases, starting by adding two extra 70 megabyte discs at each service centre.

Early Prestel service centres have been established with dual computers, one serving as a back-up to the other for security. Later centres were to have only a single computer, with the system security in the network, as explained in Chapter 10.

PRESTEL SOFTWARE

The Prestel software has been written by the BPO's internal development team, with only limited help from outside. Prestel software represents a very considerable development effort—as much as 40 man years by the end of 1979 with a lot more to come.

Originally the software was written for the Hewlett-Packard development computer. It was then re-written and improved for the GEC computer for the pilot trial. The next phase was the development of software for the Test Service. This was then extended to cater for the replicated database arrangement. It was to be extended again for the distributed database arrangement.

Inevitably within each phase there have been, and will continue to be, a number of amendments and enhancements.

The basic database maintenance and retrieval software for videotex is relatively simple. But with Prestel there are a large number of additional tasks to be considered including usage statistics, billing and payment routines, editing and bulk transfer arrangements, closed user group operations, performance testing, test monitoring and error recovery and backup procedures. It is these additional tasks which have made the Prestel software as complex as it is.

The Prestel software is written in BABBAGE, a high level language unique to the GEC 4000 series. The Prestel software also replaces the normal operating system software. For these reasons, Prestel software is not portable—it cannot be run on other computers. BPO Prestel owns the software copyright, though the overall concept is neither monopolistic nor proprietary.

BPO Prestel has succeeded in selling versions of its software to several overseas buyers: the West German Bundespost, the Dutch PTT and the Swiss PTT, for use on GEC computers. Insac, the NEB subsidiary, negotiated exclusive rights to Prestel, and succeeded in selling it in the USA during 1979. All these customers have incorporated their own modifications, some of them extensive. By the end of 1979, the value of Prestel software exports probably exceeded £1 million ($2 million). GEC's revenue from computer hardware sales was much greater.

TERMINALS

Adapted domestic TV terminals

Several classes of Prestel terminals had appeared by the start of the public service. The first of these, because it was the earliest, was the adapted domestic TV.

The original expectation of the BPO development team was that the residential market would prefer adapted domestic TV terminals rather than specially designed terminals. The team reasoned that this would make a user's purchase decision easier, and less expensive. The terminals would be supplied and maintained through the established channels.

The TV industry concurred. Moreover it preferred the idea of Prestel TVs with integral decoders designed in from the start, rather than external plug-in adaptors. With integral decoders the picture quality can be better, and the product tidier and less expensive. Another major advantage for the TV industry is that new built-in features encourage buyers to trade up. Stimulating the turnover of TV sets in the marketplace is a desirable proposition from the industry's standpoint.

The market in Britain is unusually placed to support a high rate of trading up, because it is still predominantly a rental market (although the proportion was falling, about 60% of all new colour sets going on the market at the end of the 1970s were rented). It is relatively easy for renters to exchange their TVs for a better model.

Figure 8.1 shows a typical Prestel domestic TV with integral decoder and remotely controlled keypad.

Nonetheless, external adaptors which could be plugged into the aerial socket were demonstrated during the pilot trial, and a few were used in the Test Service. And by the start of the public service there was some evidence of increasing interest in TV terminal designs fitted with sockets specifically designed to take external adaptors, to permit the same visual quality standard as with integral decoders.

Figure 8.1.   Typical domestic TV terminal.

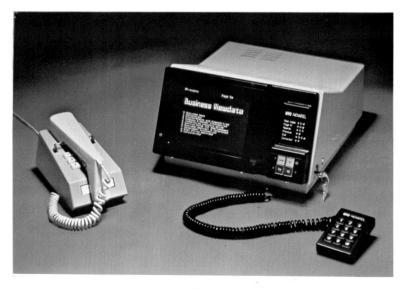

Figure 8.2.   Typical business TV terminal.

Business terminals

As soon as the interest of the business community in Prestel became apparent, the idea of purpose-designed business terminals began to grow. At first they were generally conceived as compact monochrome devices, with full alphanumeric keyboards. Like domestic terminals, they could be fitted with integral modems.

At the time of the pilot trial, the BPO waived its earlier requirement that Prestel terminals should be able to show TV pictures. By the time the Test Service began, the importance of the business terminal market was clear: 450 out of the total 700 business terminals planned were to be purpose-designed terminals.

By the start of the public service, most of the major British manufacturers—and some foreign ones (e.g. Sony, Barco)—had demonstrated business terminals for Prestel. They covered the full range of sizes, some with numeric-only keypads, and some with full alphanumeric keyboards in anticipation of the message service. Some were able to show a TV picture, and others not. But perhaps the most striking difference compared with earlier designs was the widespread use of colour. Many suppliers expected the market trend to be away from monochrome, despite colour's disadvantages of higher price and poorer definition.

Figure 8.2 shows a typical purpose-designed Prestel business terminal at the start of the public service.

The general expectation of the TV industry at the start of the public service was that most Prestel terminals delivered over the following two years would be for business use. Of these, a high proportion—perhaps the majority—would be purpose-designed.

Other terminals

Public access terminals are designed for use in places such as shops, shopping arcades, libraries, schools, Post Offices, and railway and airport terminals. There were two general classes of public access terminals in use at the time of the Test Service: free access and coin-operated.

Free access terminals were typically associated with advisory or information services, such as careers advice.

Coin-operated terminals were specially designed for use in public places such as pubs and hotel foyers, and were fitted with heavy duty enclosures. They accepted only 10p and 50p pieces, and were unable to issue change. They accounted for telephone line, connect-time and individual frame charges, together with the proprietor's profit margin.

Figure 8.3 shows a typical coin operated terminal.

Figure 8.3. Typical coin operated terminal.

Editing terminals are designed for IPs to create and maintain (*edit*) their pages on the Prestel database. The early Mark 1 terminals provided by BPO Prestel have already been described in Chapter 7. Lacking editing aids, and able only to be used online, they were slow and inefficient, but the majority of pages in the Test Service database were entered with Mark 1 editing terminals.

Since 1978, BPO Prestel has encouraged private industry to develop more advanced ('Mark 2') editing terminals for use offline. Several suppliers were able to demonstrate their designs by the start of the public service, with a number of attractive features. These included editing aids to speed up the job of data entry, local page storage, and high speed (1200 bits per second and upwards) communications for transferring completed pages to the Prestel update centre.

Dual-purpose terminals are of particular interest to the computer terminal industry. In one mode they are able to access Prestel so they can use an internal modem and can be attached to the telephone line without specific Post Office involvement. In the second mode they can act as regular VDUs with a standard 1920 character display.

Decoders

The term decoder is used to describe the device which adapts TVs to use Prestel. Decoders have often loosely been called chip sets.

Several designs were available—or becoming available—to Prestel terminal manufacturers at the start of the public service, from four leading semiconductor suppliers: GEC, GIM, Mullard and Texas Instruments. Although quite different in detail, their basic elements were not dissimilar. Figure 8.4 shows a schematic of the five basic decoder elements.

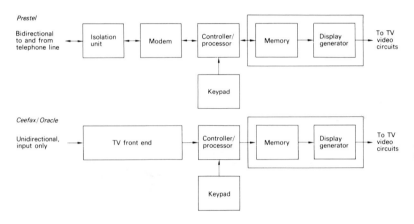

Line isolator: protects the telephone network from dangerous high voltages present in the TV.
Modem: converts the analogue telephone signals to a digital signal and vice versa.
Memory: stores data for display.
Keypad: enters characters (numerics).
Display generator: transforms characters stored in the memory to the dot patterns required for display.
Controller/input processor: controls and synchronizes the operation of the components, processes incoming signals and stores them in memory.

Figure 8.4.   Basic elements of Prestel and Ceefax/Oracle decoders.

There is a high degree of commonality between Prestel and Ceefax/Oracle teletext decoders, as emphasized in the figure. This commonality springs from the use of similar display and transmission specifications, and is a feature which the suppliers have been anxious to exploit.

Decoders can be fitted to a terminal either internally or externally, and the modem element can be integral or separate from the decoder. Thus manufacturers have several choices of arrangement. In Britain, the arrangement favoured at the time of the Test Service was for integral decoders fitted internally, for reasons which have already been explained. That the BPO has given permission for modems to be integral, and for terminals to be attached to the telephone network without their direct involvement, has meant a significant break with previous policy.

The price of decoders is critical to Prestel's success, particularly in the residential market. Their prices are highly volume sensitive, rather like electronic calculators. Prices acceptable to a mass market will only be achieved with mass market volumes, in the absence of subsidies or major supplier investments.

Early Prestel decoders were sold by the semiconductor suppliers for around £300 ($600) each. The price halved as soon as they were being manufactured in volumes of hundreds. When production volumes reach thousands per month, the semiconductor suppliers have predicted that decoder prices will fall to around £15 ($30) each, including the modem.

But the cost of testing decoders and fitting them to TVs will mean a higher incremental price in the marketplace, as shown in Figure 8.5.

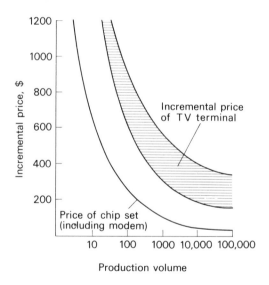

Figure 8.5.   Incremental price of Prestel TV terminal with integral decoder.

CHAPTER 9

PRESTEL COSTS AND REVENUES

REVENUE FLOWS

Main revenue flows

As a commercial service, Prestel is designed to earn profits for its suppliers from revenues which users should be prepared and willing to pay. This commercial promise is based on the expectation of a mass market. The public service tariffs described in this chapter have been set with that in mind.

Direct subsidies have not been part of the Prestel plan. The service has meant investment by all the main suppliers, but in principle they are no different to those in any other business venture.

The pricing strategy for the publicly available service is one of payment by usage. For residential users, no subscription fee is arranged. (Business users pay a small subscription.) Figure 9.1 shows the main revenue flows in the Prestel public service. In summary:

Users pay BPO Prestel for connect-time (1), IPs for frame accesses when charged (2), PO Telecommunications for the telephone usage at normal rates (3), and the TV industry for adapted TVs (4). In return, users receive the benefits of the service.
BPO Prestel pays operating costs and overheads (5). It also pays PO Telecommunications for telephone usage at normal rates (6). In return, it receives connect-time charges from users (1), and storage charges from IPs (7).
IPs pay BPO Prestel service and storage charges, called plain 'storage' charges (7), and PO Telecommunications for telephone services (8). They also pay the costs of their own database design and maintenance. In return, IPs receive frame access revenues (2) from users.

The TV industry pays for terminal development, production and marketing. In return it receives revenues from users (4).

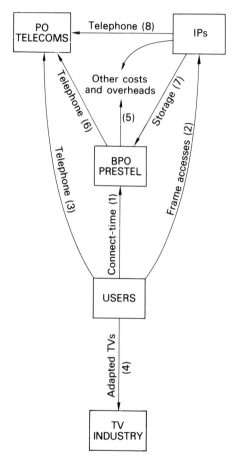

Figure 9.1. Main Prestel revenue flows.

BPO Prestel receives no credit from telephone traffic revenues in order to avoid criticism of unfair advantage as explained in Chapter 6. One consequence of this is that BPO Prestel's tariffs are inevitably set at a higher level than would otherwise be necessary.

The commercial basis of the Prestel operation is highly volume sensitive. The following is a highly simplified analysis of the values of the main revenue flows in Figure 9.1. There are a number of underlying assumptions. The most important of these is the assumption of ten service centres, each with a replicated database updated from a single centre. Each service centre is assumed to be configured with 300 ports, giving a total of 3000 user ports in the network.

The revenues are calculated using tariffs and prices applying at the end of 1979.

Charge rates

(1) *Connect-time charge*

The charge unit is 3p (6 cents). One charge unit buys 3 minutes at cheap times and 1 minute at standard times. Standard times are 08.00–18.00 on weekdays; cheap times apply otherwise.

(2) *Frame access charge*

Frame access charges are in accordance with the prices set by individual IPs, though within agreed limits (0–50p in small steps). Each access to a frame incurs a charge equivalent to the frame price, even though the same frame may be accessed many times in a session.

(3) *Telephone charge*

The telephone charge unit is 3p (6 cents). The telephone connection to Prestel is at normal rates, and usually at local call rates. The 3p charge unit buys the following local call durations:

2 minutes at peak periods 09.00–13.00, weekdays.
3 minutes at standard periods 08.00–09.00 and 13.00–18.00, weekdays.
12 minutes at other periods on weekdays, and all times at weekends.

(4) *Adapted TVs*

The premium price for an adapted TV will be around £150 ($300) inclusive of installation and connection charges when the terminal installed base has reached the 300,000 level. The equivalent annual rental or depreciation is about £1 ($2) per week.

COSTS AND REVENUES FOR SERVICE PROVIDERS

BPO Prestel costs and revenues

The cost of a Prestel service centre is expected to be roughly £500,000 ($1 million) per annum. This is inclusive of capital costs, running costs and overheads, and includes a proportion of the costs of the corporate HQ, the update centre and R&D.

The revenue from IPs' storage charges (7) at the update centre is about £2 million per annum—equivalent to £200,000 ($400,000) per service centre in a ten-service-centre operation.

In order to balance costs with revenues, an additional revenue of £300,000 per annum per centre is required from connect-time charges. To make an adequate profit, the revenue from connect-time charges should be, say, £500,000 per service centre.

What should the connect-time charge rate be to generate this level of revenue? First, the number of port hours which should be available from a service centre is around 500,000 per year. This assumes that the 300 ports are fully utilized for the equivalent of 5.5 hours in every 24, for 300 days per year. So the price per port hour to generate £500,000 should be about £1 ($2). This is about 1.6p per minute (3.2 cents).

IP costs and revenues

An IP's cost of frame maintenance varies greatly according to the number of frames, frame update frequency, the expense of information sources and so forth. What might a typical cost be? Assume an IP maintains 1000 frames at the update centre, with weekly updates to each frame. The average inclusive cost per frame will work out at about £24 ($48) per frame per year (service and storage charges payable to BPO Prestel are about £8, editing costs about £8, and overheads and promotion about £8).

Table 9.1. Average yearly number of accesses per frame

One Prestel service centre generates 30 million port minutes per annum:

300 ports used 300 days for 5.5 hours on average
= approx. 30 million port minutes per annum

At 4 frames per minute (one every 15 seconds) the number of frame accesses at 10 service centres is:

30 million × 10 × 4 = 1200 million per annum

With 250,000 different frames, the average number of accesses per frame is:

$$\frac{1200 \text{ million}}{250,000} = 4800 \text{ per annum}$$

For the IP to profit, the revenue generation per frame should be at least £30 per annum. The average frame on the database is accessed in this ten-service-centres operation model 4800 times per year as shown in Table 9.1.

Assuming the IP's frames are each accessed the average number of times, the frame price should be set at £30/4800 to make a profit, i.e. about 0.6p (1.2 cents) each.

Of course, the pricing policy of individual IPs will vary. Some may cut their prices in the hope of gaining greater frame use. Others will raise their prices, particularly for high value frames. Some will not charge a price per frame at all, choosing to give their information away free of charge for promotional purposes.

Accounting and billing

BPO Prestel records the details of each IP and its frame numbers at the update centre, and of each user and his access statistics at the service centres to which the user is connected.

BPO Prestel bills IPs monthly according to the charges detailed above. It credits them for revenues collected on their behalf, less a factoring charge (e.g. 5% of revenues). IPs' accounts show a breakdown of gross access statistics by frame, not by user.

USER SESSION COSTS

Residential users

Residential users pay for Prestel in four separate ways:

for connect-time to the database
for frame accesses
for telephone charges
for adapted TV terminals.

Assume that a typical residential user connects to Prestel once per day, each time for a session of about 3 minutes, mainly in the evening. The total weekly connect-time is about 20 minutes, and the total number of frames viewed, assuming one every 15 seconds, is 80.

The following approximate costs will apply:

connect-time, say	30p
frame accesses, say	50p
telephone charges, say	20p
TV set amortization, say	100p
	200p equivalent to £2 or about $4

At 20 minutes each per week, and assuming a smooth demand for Prestel (most unlikely in practice), the number of residential users who can be supported per service centre with a capacity of 500,000 port hours per year is:

$$\frac{500,000 \times 60}{20 \times 52} \approx 30,000 \qquad \text{i.e. 100 users per port}$$

The key figure is £2 total user charge for roughly 20 minutes usage. That is roughly 10p (20 cents) per minute. At first sight this looks relatively expensive: it is about ten times the cost per minute of a movie ticket. But there will be many occasions when the information to be culled will be well worth the price.

The above figures are very approximate. In practice the overall charge for Prestel usage will vary widely, according to the time of the day and the price of pages accessed. Here are some guidelines:

The minimum charge for a session will be 6p. This will be for a 1 minute session involving only a single charge unit for telephone usage and connect-time, both of 3p. It assumes that all frames accessed are zero priced.

The minimum charge for a 2 minute session at peak times of the day will be 9p. The minimum charge unit of 3p for the telephone will buy 2 minutes usage, and connect-time will cost 2 units of 3p each. Again this assumes that the frames accessed are free.

In the evenings, the minimum priced 12 minute session will cost 15p. The telephone will cost 3p and connect-time will cost 12p. If 4 average frames of about 0.6p each are accessed per minute during the session, the total cost will be more than 40p.

One interesting outcome of the average residential user's expense of £2 per week shown above is that half the total revenues arising from the Prestel service accrue to the TV industry.

All the figures set out previously make no allowance for VAT (value added tax). In Britain, VAT was set at 15% in 1979—high enough to make a significant impact on the estimations. To a residential user, all the Prestel charges are subject to VAT, with the exception of frame charges. HM Customs and Excise agreed in the Summer of 1979 that, like newsprint, frame access charges should be zero-rated for VAT.

Business users

Compared with the average residential usage, business usage will be more intensive and the charge rate per unit time almost certainly higher as a result of peak hour usage and more expensive frames. Again, compared with residential usage, there will be fewer users per port.

SERVICE INVESTMENT

The ten-service-centre operation described above indicates how service providers ought to be able to cover their costs—and make profits—at prices which the market might be expected to pay. But the key assumption is the ten-service-centre operation. Conceivably, this is sufficient to support over a quarter of a million residential users.

Admittedly this is a very simplistic analysis. It takes no account of the many detailed variations in costs and prices which undoubtedly will occur, for example response frames and factoring charges. Nonetheless it is useful as a first approximation. The question for service providers is how long it will be before that number of users are connected, because during the interim the service providers will be carrying their share of the investments.

Beyond about ten service centres, the rate of return for the service suppliers should grow impressively. From the IPs' standpoint, promotional costs will rise; but their other costs are relatively independent of volume, unlike newsprint.

CHAPTER 10

DEVELOPMENT PLANS AND PROSPECTS

SHORT TERM EXPANSION PLANS

Service centres in major towns

As explained in Chapter 6, BPO Prestel's strategy is one of rapid service expansion. That means bringing Prestel quickly within reach of a high proportion of the population, and keeping the capacity for supporting terminals well up with the demand. There is a good deal of uncertainty about where the demand will arise and how fast it will grow. And service provision can entail a lead time of twelve months and more—for computer service centre installation, trunk connections, any modifications to local exchanges, and even the provision of additional local exchange lines for businesses. Consequently BPO Prestel has to plan a capital spending programme well ahead of demand, choosing areas where it is confident that demand will materialize.

BPO Prestel allocated a capital budget of £23 million in 1978 mainly for spending on equipment for the Test Service and the early public service, to permit the opening of centres in over a dozen major cities as shown in Table 10.1.

According to this plan, issued at the end of 1979, over 60% of the national telephone-owning population was to be within local call reach of a Prestel centre by the end of 1980, and sufficient capacity was to be available for almost half a million terminals. Although the table does not show it, the plan called for the installation of more than 20 computers and a total of several thousand ports.

Where there appears to be demand in an area out of local call reach of a Prestel centre, but the demand is insufficient to justify the immediate installation of a centre, BPO Prestel is unlikely to encourage STD access to a remote centre. It will prefer to install local concentrators attached to high capacity trunk lines connected back to the nearest centre. Indeed, some of the smaller cities listed in Table 10.1 were to be serviced at first through concentrators in this way.

Beyond the end of 1980, BPO Prestel has remained consistently optimistic about its plans for extending the service. In May 1979 it was predicting that the number of ports' available by mid-1981 would reach 12,600—adequate to support, in BPO Prestel's view, over 1 million terminals.

Beyond that, the plan was not firm. But there remained an intention to increase both the capacity in the population areas already covered, and to extend Prestel's availability to a higher proportion of the telephone-owning population.

Table 10.1. Summary of proposed short term expansion plans for Prestel

Location	Expected start date of service
London	September 1979[a]
Birmingham	December 1979
Nottingham	December 1979
Edinburgh	February 1980
Glasgow	February 1980
Manchester	March 1980
Liverpool	March 1980
Luton	June 1980
Reading	June 1980
Sevenoaks	June 1980
Brighton	June 1980
Leeds	July 1980
Newcastle	July 1980
Cardiff	August 1980
Bristol	August 1980
Bournemouth	August 1980
Chelmsford	September 1980
Norwich	September 1980

[a] This was the opening date of the first centre; other London centres were due to open from early 1980.

Extending database capacity

At the start of the public service, the database capacity available to IPs was 180,000 frames. It was already a service constraint. At that time a demand existed from IPs for more space than was available, and many other potential IPs (BPO Prestel claimed over 100) were queueing up waiting for space.

To alleviate the situation, BPO Prestel was planning to double the storage space available. This would be achieved by adding new high performance disc storage devices at the service centres without jeopardizing the system performance.

To install and fill the extra capacity will take time. Prestel users are unlikely to benefit until beyond 1981.

Supplying and connecting terminals

The short supply of terminals at the start of the public service was a source of concern to BPO Prestel and IPs alike. If this shortage were to persist, it could lead to an embarrassing volume of surplus port capacity if BPO Prestel were to open centres as planned.

There were several reasons for the shortage. One important reason was delays over agreement to the final details of the decoder specification, still under discussion in 1979. Perhaps most important, however, was the TV manufacturers' reluctance to invest in Prestel's future by placing large orders for decoder chip sets on the semiconductor suppliers in the absence of their own large orders for completed terminals.

But there were some signs late in 1979 that the situation was indeed about to improve. The estimates given by BREMA and TEMA for terminal supply in 1980 were respectively 50,000 and 30,000. Most of these were expected to be used by the business community.

One benefit to users that surplus computer capacity, if it occurred, would bring was high port availability. This would ensure that the number of attempted connections greeted by the busy signal would be minimized.

Encouraging the demand

For Prestel to achieve rapid penetration requires awareness of what it is and what it can do, particularly among the residential community. (At the start of the public service, people's awareness of Prestel was not high: only 9% in a poll of 2000 had heard of it, compared with around 30% for Ceefax and Oracle.)

To improve awareness requires a lot of publicity. The plan was for a publicity campaign to begin in spring 1980, coincident with an expected improvement in the availability of TV terminals. The three Prestel service participants were to co-operate in a joint campaign with a £1 million budget, as well as conducting their own separate campaigns. The purpose of the campaigns was both to attract new users and to increase their usage of the service.

NEW PRESTEL SERVICES

Message services

Some caution is needed over predicting Prestel's future beyond the short term expansion plans described above. At the start of the public service, Prestel's success was still not certain. But if the experience of the critical early years of the 1980s is encouraging, BPO Prestel will want to press ahead with new services—messages, computation and software distribution. It is also likely to be interested in extending the scope of Prestel, for example with dedicated closed user group operations.

Response frame messages have been a part of the Test Service and early public service. Users have been able to complete response frames put up by IPs and return them to a message pool ready for collection by IPs later. But response frames have had practical limitations. BPO Prestel has said that the next steps will be to improve the response frame facility and to extend the message services to permit user-to-user messages.

The planned improvements to the response frame facility aim at increasing the capacity of the message pool, and permitting IPs to scrutinize more easily their messages using remote terminals.

User-to-user messages have not been part of the Test Service or early public service. Although user-to-user messages of both the store and forward and conversational type were demonstrated during the pilot trial, they were removed for simplicity and to avoid the danger of jeopardizing the system performance in its all-important information retrieval mode. But it has remained BPO Prestel's intention to re-introduce user-to-user messages at some stage.

The emphasis is likely to be on store and forward (mailbox) messages. The principle is similar to the response frame facility. Recipients need to be notified of the awaiting message, in order to retrieve it.

The concept raises some interesting questions to do with message preparation, storage and collection. For example, will the sender or the recipient pay for storage? How will the recipient be identified by the sender, and how will a recipient be informed reliably that a message is waiting? The technical problems here are quite complex.

The ramifications of a mailbox type message service could be very considerable. For example, if it were to connect with the telex network, it could dramatically increase the availability of that service.

With conversational messages the storage time is reduced to zero, and messages flow back and forth between sender and recipient as in a telephone conversation. Conversational messages were demonstrated during the pilot trial, with each user's display split to show outgoing and incoming messages simultaneously.

Message services on Prestel are likely to prove increasingly important in the future, particularly those of the response frame type for applications such as teleshopping and reservations. When the replicated database arrangement is eventually superseded by a distributed database network (see below), BPO Prestel's intention is that comprehensive message services should be built into the design. But the task will not be easy. It will prove to be a difficult undertaking in its own right, and the question of whether and how to integrate Prestel message services with other electronic mail systems already at the planning stage will not be easy to answer.

Computation

Computation was demonstrated on Prestel during the pilot trial. However, because computation makes relatively heavy demands on the processor, the facility was withdrawn for the Test Service and early public service to prevent jeopardizing the computers' information retrieval performance.

If the public service experience confirms that spare processing capacity is available, a computation service is likely to be introduced, at least to test the market response.

The likelihood is that popular programs will be stored on service centre computers for use in the same way as with time sharing computer service bureaux. Users will enter parameters through their terminals in response to screen prompts.

Some of the likely applications are mortgage and taxation calculations. Other programs might be designed to help with education; in mathematics and physics training, for example.

Software distribution

Software distribution was demonstrated on Prestel in 1978, though it was not available for the Test Service or early public service. The idea is that computer programs, rather than information intelligible to a person, are stored on the database pages. They can be selected by a user just like ordinary information pages, and loaded downline for local use, for example into a personal computer.

To be practical, the software must be capable of being run either on a variety of computers or on one popular range. A realistic payment mechanism is also necessary. Compared with regular information, software on Prestel will be of high intrinsic value, and somewhat involatile. For this reason there has been interest in the idea of software which disables itself after a specified period following its distribution.

Some of the likely applications include sophisticated games for the home, and simple application packages for small business users such as payroll and accounts. The first demonstration of software distribution through Prestel was by CAP (a major British software house) which demonstrated downloading of a 'MicroCobol' program to permit high speed access to a portion of the travel timetable pages of ABC, one of the more experienced IPs.

Dedicated closed user group operations

An indication of the extent to which the market for Prestel in Britain was already segmenting at the end of 1979 was given by BPO Prestel's announcement of its interest in establishing a closed user group operation using a dedicated computer in London. Invitations were issued to lease capacity in lots of 25,000 frames and 20 ports for a period of 2 years, at prices subject to negotiation.

This move was probably stimulated by the demand for closed user group services on its publicly available service centres. The single dedicated closed user group computer was expected to be sited in central London, with access from anywhere within the United Kingdom through either the public switched telephone network or private networks.

Access to Prestel information from overseas

By the start of the public service, there was a considerable amount of interest in the idea of accessing information stored on Prestel from overseas. BPO Prestel was anxious to test the market, and learn about the problems and pitfalls. Following a study carried out during 1979, it agreed to launch a one year trial* starting early in 1980, using the name *Prestel International*. Users in seven countries (Australia, Holland, Switzerland, Sweden, the USA, West Germany and the UK itself) would be able to access a specially prepared database at the original Test Service Centre in Gresham Street, London.

The aims of Prestel International would be to explore the type of information wanted, how often it would be wanted, and at what price. It would also be an opportunity to help resolve some of the many technical, social and legal issues arising from international database access. It would be aimed solely at business users, particularly multinationals, and would include closed user groups.

If the trial proves successful, it could be followed by a larger scale service.

NETWORK AND TERMINAL DEVELOPMENTS

Distributed database network

As explained in Chapter 8, Prestel's replicated database arrangement is expected to be superseded by a distributed database network in which databases at individual service centres will no longer be identical. The distributed database design should lead to a number of advantages. The page capacity of the system

---

* Actually begun in February 1980.

should be greatly increased. The information needs of local communities should be improved. IPs should find it easier to update their pages. And it is BPO Prestel's intention that the message services should be greatly enhanced.

The details were not settled at the end of 1979. However, under the new arrangement each database will probably offer a mix of local and national information. Users wishing to access information held at a remote service centre will be able to do so. The idea is that complete indexes will be carried at all the service centres, with a facility to transfer data from remote service centres—called 'rare' data—built into the design.

The system will require a considerable amount of wholly new software to be written and tested. Even if a start were to be made in 1980, the distributed database network would be unlikely to be available before 1983.

Computer centres

Early Prestel service centres were established with dual computers, one serving as a back-up to the other and able to be manually switched in in the event of the failure of the first. Later centres are expected to be equipped with only a single computer. The system security will be in the network. The autodiallers on the TV terminals are being built to hold two Prestel telephone numbers, for the local Prestel centre and the adjacent centre respectively. The autodialler will alternate from one number to the other automatically on alternative calls. If one is busy or unobtainable, the other is tried next.

These later service centres are expected to be configured with up to 400 ports each, in anticipation of the computers' ability to handle that number of simultaneous users. The storage capacity at each service centre will probably be raised as well, eventually to over a million pages.

Terminal developments

Rapid development on the terminal front can be expected following the early public service. These developments will result from increasing market demand and increasing supplier competition.

The first priority will be to extend the range of terminals available to meet a variety of market needs, from full size, upmarket colour domestic receivers, to small compact monochrome sets for use on a desk top or in a kitchen. Both colour and monochrome will be featured, probably with increasing emphasis on colour; colour's attractiveness will often overcome its disadvantages of higher price and somewhat inferior definition. The presence and absence of both TV and teletext capabilities will be features of the growing range of terminals.

The second priority will be to make improvements in detail design to give a competitive edge. Keypads and keyboards will be areas of particular interest. The design emphasis will be on improving ease of use, reducing keying errors and providing features such as programmable keys to permit quick access to regularly used page numbers. The amount of internal terminal memory offered will be increased to permit the storing of multiple pages, to save users' time and money.

The most important priority will be to increase terminal production volumes and reduce prices. The suppliers have said repeatedly that when the market can be seen to be materializing they will be ready to produce terminals in quantity. The British market for colour TVs alone was running at over 150,000 per month at the end of the 1970s. If just 10% of these were fitted with Prestel decoders, the premium price of a Prestel TV could drop as low as 15% of the regular price, or about £75 ($150) for a fully featured TV at 1979 prices. This is no more than the reduction in the real term price of a regular TV set which can be confidently predicted in the early 1980s as a result of design and production improvements.

A further priority for the terminal industry will be to provide printer and storage attachments. Several types of printers have been under development for Prestel, some using aluminium coated electro-sensitive paper, and others plain paper. With volume production, the price of these printers could drop below £100 ($200). An alternative to printing pages will be to record them. It will be possible to use ordinary audio cassette recorders, with only minor modifications, to record pages for later playback. One side of a C60 cassette could hold over 300 Prestel pages.

FUTURE OF PRESTEL

The willingness of all three main service providers to invest further in Prestel will depend on the outcome of the early public service. The first two years of the 1980s will be critical.

What is the response likely to be? In 1978, BPO Prestel was prepared to predict several million users in Britain by 1983. By the end of 1979 that was already looking rather optimistic, though there were still almost as many predictions as there were observers prepared to make them.

From the supply viewpoint, one million terminals by 1983 seemed well within the bounds of possibility. The TV industry alone could probably produce that number of terminals (the *annual* production rate of colour TVs for the domestic market at the end of the 1970s was around one and a half million), and BPO Prestel could probably install enough ports (particularly if most users were residential: one million residential terminals could be serviced through fifty centres, assuming 200 ports per centre and 100 terminals per port).

But is one million terminals a reasonable expectation from the demand viewpoint? At the end of 1979, it looked unrealistically high. The signs were that the residential market would grow at a relatively slow rate—perhaps to around 100,000 or 200,000 terminals in use by 1983. The price of Prestel, the impending recession, the incompleteness of the database, and the apparent advantages of teletext (cheaper to install and use) would see to that. It seemed that the business market would prove to be more important in this early period of Prestel's growth—certainly in terms of usage, if not in terms of numbers of terminals installed.

Although less sanguine than BPO Prestel's, the market projection just described still amounts to a substantial business. More importantly, it should be sufficiently large for Prestel service participants to start making a return on their investments.

Beyond 1983, it was possible to predict that significant new pressures would be shaping the market—though the precise nature and extent of these pressures still remained unclear.

Part 3

WORLDWIDE VIDEOTEX DEVELOPMENTS

trials and service plans

CHAPTER 11

DEVELOPMENTS IN EUROPE

WIDESPREAD INTEREST IN EUROPE

Videotex activity in a number of countries

In Europe the main focus of videotex activities is on publicly available services. Here it is the PTTs—the monopoly telecommunications operators—which are the prime movers. Table 11.1 shows seven European countries with active plans as at mid-1979. At that time, five of these countries had announced their plans for public market trials. The consistent pattern of development was for a private market trial (*pilot trial*) to be followed by a public market trial, then a public service. Both Britain and France were formally committed to public services, and there was a high probability that the other countries would follow suit.

Apart from these, other European countries were following videotex developments closely with a view to starting their own trials in due course. Examples included Austria, Belgium, Denmark, Italy, Norway and Spain.

Table 11.1. European countries actively planning publicly available videotex

	Name of service	Market trial	Public Service[a]
Britain	Prestel	1978/80	1979[b]
France	Teletel	1980/81	1982
West Germany	Bildschirmtext	1980/81	1982
Holland	Viditel[c]	1980/81	1982
Finland	Telset	1979/80	1980
Switzerland	Videotex	1980/81	1983
Sweden	DataVision	—	1983

[a] Likely date.
[b] Actual date.
[c] Renamed around the end of 1979.

The interest in videotex shared by the European PTTs springs from common aims: to stimulate traffic growth on the telephone network, and to position themselves for the anticipated surge in electronic communications in the future. The PTTs' prime interest lies in the potentially huge residential market, particularly in Britain, France and West Germany, which are high population countries. But the PTTs' interest is not restricted just to the residential marketplace. Some PTTs (the Swedish PTT is an example) see the business market as more attractive—particularly in the short term—because it will be less price sensitive.

There has been continuing concern among the service suppliers, echoed by many industry observers, about the readiness of the residential market to accept both the concept of videotex, and the price levels at which services can be made available assuming commercially realistic operations with today's technology. A service directly subsidized by a state is of course another matter, though for regulatory and monopolistic reasons direct state subsidies are in fact unlikely. They will remain unlikely if the European political climate apparent at the end of the 1970s persists, with a shift in favour of free enterprise and reduced state intervention. However, it is also true that many PTTs are in a position to commit major long term investments, perhaps beyond what would be regarded as justifiable by the private sector.

Boundaries of telecommunications monopolies

In virtually all European countries, the telephone network is regarded as a natural monopoly. The PTTs are entrusted by the state with the task of operating the network and expanding its services to meet changing user requirements, such as in the area of data communications. In many countries, the PTT is directly responsible to a Ministry of Telecommunications which determines policy and investment priorities. In this case, investment capital is provided directly by the government. Elsewhere, the PTT is an independent, state-owned Corporation whose monopoly powers are derived from Government legislation, or an assumed historical monopoly position. The monopolies embrace physical network provision including trunk lines, exchanges and links to individual subscribers' premises. But they also extend beyond mere network provisioning to include the provision of private leased circuits that pass over the public domain; the provision of value added services on leased or switched telegraph or telephone lines; regulation of the approval and connection of devices to the public switched telephone network; and regulation by adjusting tariffs.

Finally the PTTs have the right to decide when and how a new service will be introduced. They can, for example, restrict the use of the voice network for data transmission. Most European PTTs are now developing dedicated public data networks (PDNs) using both circuit- and packet-switched technology. The PTTs may raise the tariffs and restrict the availability of leased private lines to encourage traffic on to the PDNs. The PTTs recognize the large potential market for business electronic mail, and are engaged in the preparation of a teletex standard aimed at enabling terminals manufactured by different suppliers to communicate over the public telephone networks.

The PTTs' inability to provide a full range of data services will be one of the key issues in the growing debate over PTT monopolies in Europe. Private industry has pressed for a liberalization of the monopolies for many years, though it was only towards the end of the 1970s that governments began seriously to review the monopoly positions.

The obligations arising from a national monopoly are a principal factor in determining the structure of new services. In particular the PTTs are obliged to meet the demands of both large and small users on the broadest geographic and usage bases.

For example, the new packet-switching services being introduced in some countries at the end of the 1970s have tariffs which do not differentiate between the localities of the users, and attempt not to discourage the occasional user in favour of the large customer. The result is that new services are often overpriced because they assume nationwide traffic long before demand is established outside major business centres.

Often in the past, European PTTs have been too preoccupied with return on investment to underprice new services in order to stimulate demand. Their marketing policies have frequently served to discourage even the existing latent demand, and goes no way towards stimulating new business.

This picture has begun to change as PTTs have become aware of commercial practices in other industries, especially data processing. In the past, the PTTs were not under pressure to stimulate the telephone market. Quite the reverse was true, due to the inability of PTTs to keep up with growing demand. More recently, even in telephony, the PTTs have been promoting their own services. The marketing skills acquired in this area have slowly been diffusing into data services.

In most European countries the question of media control is becoming a cause of increasing concern. This has been spurred by two main factors. The first is the rapid development of technology permitting the advent of new services and threatening established ones. The second is the public's increasing concern over issues such as privacy and state control. The issues are very broad. They include the control of information sources, the control of distribution media, and editorial and privacy issues.

Some European countries, notably Norway and Sweden, inaugurated state commissions to examine these issues in the late 1970s. Generally the aims of such state commissions are to seek ways of ensuring the protection of the interests of individuals through a continuing balance between state and private information sources, and a continuing respect of individuals' right to privacy.

The fading boundary between telecommunications and data processing has been much discussed in recent years—the so called 'convergence' phenomenon. Of similar importance is the fading boundary between telecommunications and broadcasting. In some European countries, broadcasting is a separately controlled part of telecommunications. For example, in France the PTT has a monopoly of point-to-point telecommunications, and the TDF (Telediffussion de France, the state monopoly broadcasting company) for broadcasting. In Britain, broadcasting is a specific exclusion to the BPO's privilege as set out in the Post Office Act. The BBC, which supplies two television channels, and the IBA which supplies one independent channel, each have a separate charter of operation from the BPO, renewable every three years by the Home Office permitting them to broadcast.

Technical similarities and differences in system designs

From a technical standpoint, the systems under development at the time of writing have a number of similarities in common. All, with one exception, are based on Prestel's display and transmission standard. The exception is in France where the Antiope standard is used. All are alphamosaic systems, displaying six colours as well as black and white. All employ a display grid of 40 characters per row and 24 rows per frame (25 with Antiope), with a data transmission speed of 1200/75 bits per second. All offer simple selection of information pages from numbered menu choices.

But there are significant differences too. For example, Prestel uses replicated databases in its early public service. Change information is transmitted from an update centre to each service centre where a copy of the replicated database is maintained. West Germany's Bildschirmtext has been designed to permit information retrieval from databases at the service centres, and also on remote 'host' computers. In France's design for Teletel, the intention is for information to be stored solely on databases distributed among remote host computers, accessible through the Transpac public packet switching network. For Prestel, the BPO is permitting integral modems, built inside terminals. Other PTTs favour external modems.

To gain a head start with their videotex trials, the PTTs in West Germany, Holland and Switzerland bought Prestel software and knowhow from the BPO, but before the end of 1979 they had already made extensive alterations, and continued allegiance to Prestel was not certain. The PTTs in other countries, such as Finland and Sweden, adopted the Prestel terminal and transmission standards but developed their own software and introduced their own innovations.

There has been much international debate on the question of videotex standards. At first the differences between Prestel and Antiope, and the prospects for a compromise, were the main focus of attention. Prestel benefited from its existing strong user lobby and its low cost emphasis, Antiope from its advantages of superior display flexibility. More recently other systems, notably Telidon, have gained attention too (see Chapter 2).

FRANCE'S TELETEL AND ELECTRONIC DIRECTORY

Telecommunications and broadcasting environment

In the past, and still to some extent today, France's relatively inefficient telecommunications network has been a source of some concern and embarrassment. But this position has been changing rapidly. During the sixth national plan (1971 to 1975) 100 billion francs—over $20 billion—were poured into the telecommunications business. As a result, one of the highest growth rates ever recorded in any country was achieved; exchange lines and telephone traffic grew at 18% and 15% per annum respectively.

The plan is to continue this acceleration of telecommunications developments between 1976 and 1982 in the seventh national plan. The target is the provision of almost 20 million telephone lines with a telephone density of virtually 100 per 100 households.

Compared with other European countries, France probably has an even keener national recognition of the need for strong and co-ordinated telecommunications developments. The potential impact on the French economy and social structure of low cost computing power distributed and linked through national data networks achieved public recognition, and even notoriety, following the publication in early 1978 of the Nora and Minc report. In their report, Nora and Minc coined the term *Telematique*, the combination of computers with telecommunications, to describe the use of widespread distributed computing networks. Telematique, they suggested, would revolutionize society in many ways. The right government policy was seen as critical to gain the benefits and avoid the drawbacks.

The report went on to recommend government action, calling for heavy investment in those manufacturing industries which, when computerized, would be most likely to become competitive in the world market. A key emphasis was on the need for large volume production. The plan recognized that on the one hand Telematique would lead to dramatic increases in productivity and industry, and on the other hand the opportunity to save French jobs through a concerted export effort on information technology related products.

The French are intent on emulating Japanese manufacturing and marketing methods, and the government intends to provide the money to create the mass markets for the products in question. As a consequence there is a great deal of activity in a number of areas including telex, teletex, high speed digital networks, packet-switching, satellite transmission, new TV services, and new graphical communication services including facsimile and videotex.

Tictac, Titan and Antiope

Tictac was designed as a very simple two-way videotex system using a touch-tone telephone set, with 10 digits and 2 complementary keys, connected to a monochrome TV receiver through a low speed modem. It was conceived by CNET in 1971 and demonstrated in the mid-1970s.

By then, the need had been clearly perceived for a common standard for both one-way (broadcast) and two-way (interactive) TV based information services. The result was Antiope, developed at the CCETT—the Centre Commun d'Etudes de Television et de Telecommunications—the French PTT and TDF joint research establishment. The Antiope standard covers transmission, coding and display specifications. Consequently both teletext and videotex systems are often referred to in France as Antiope. More properly they are called broadcast videotex and interactive videotex respectively.

Antiope was designed independent of, and later than, Tictac. Its broad-based design concept and greatly enhanced capabilities compared with Tictac led to its adoption in 1977 as the foundation for France's videotex plans. Besides being suitable as the basis for both broadcast and interactive services, Antiope offered independence between transmission coding and display, together with a wide range of display character sets.

By 1978 the CCETT was able to demonstrate adapted TVs using the Antiope standard to access an experimental database called Titan. From that basis, the PTT began vigorously to pursue its plan for a public videotex service to be called Teletel.

Teletel trial plans

Teletel is the name of the French PTT's interactive videotex using the Antiope standard. At the time of writing, a public market trail was planned to start towards the end of 1980, and to last at least 18 months. There was a firm commitment to follow this with a public service, possibly starting in 1982.

The Teletel market trial will take place in a suburb of South West Paris called Velizy, close to Versailles. There will be around 2000–2500 participants, mostly from the residential sector. A variety of terminals will be tested, including colour and monochrome types of various sizes with both internal and external decoders.

The main purposes of the trial are to explore service parameters, such as terminal design and applications; to measure the market response; to evaluate the economics of the service; and to predict the potential of Teletel in terms of applications, market demand, geographical spread and growth rate.

Both information retrieval and message services will be available during the trial. To retrieve information, the participants will be able to use the tree searching method with numbered menu choices. They will also be able to retrieve information by 'keyword, using full alphanumeric keyboards. Thus it will be possible to compare these two access methods during the trial. The type of information which will be accessible will include local information, consumer rights and bank statements. Over 150 information providers will be involved, most of whom had been identified by the end of 1979, and were in the process of agreeing their contracts with the PTT.

A comprehensive message service will be part of the trial. The participants will be able to send messages to each other as well as to information providers. Message applications will include orders to mail order companies, and reservations for trains, shows and package tours. A payment facility will be included. Some of the terminals are to be fitted with card readers for this purpose.

A key feature of Teletel is that databases will be held on external host computers, remote from the Teletel service centres (see Chapter 2). The databases will be connected to the Teletel centres using the Transpac packet-switching network. The database information will be maintained at the host computers by the information providers.

The overall system architecture envisages users' terminals being connected via the regular telephone network to the Teletel centres. The Teletel centres—the local access centres—will serve as intelligent concentrators. They will not be the repository of large scale information. They will be used by the PTT to store administration information such as subscriber details, high-level indexes and messages. The concentrators will also perform the task of transmission speed and protocol conversion, and data network access (see Figure 11.1).

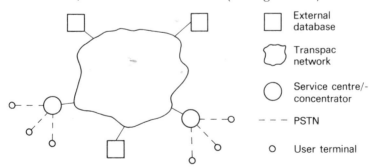

	External database
	Transpac network
	Service centre/-concentrator
- - -	PSTN
o	User terminal

Figure 11.1.   Teletel network schematic.

At the end of 1979 the service charging arrangements were still not clear. However, the use of remote databases will introduce some complications. Some information providers will wish to provide free information right up to the concentrators, whereas others will wish to provide free information, but expect users to bear the cost of transmission. The use of Transpac will ensure that transmission tariffs are distance-independent.

Electronic telephone directory

In parallel with the Teletel trial at Velizy, the French PTT is planning a separate trial of its electronic telephone directory. Like Teletel, it will use technology based on Antiope. A preliminary trial will start in the summer of 1980 in St Malo, to be followed by a full-scale trial involving all the telephone subscribers in an entire region, at Ille-et-Vilaine in the greater Rennes area (Brittany).

The plan is for the full-scale trial to begin at the end of 1981, and for all the 270,000 subscribers in the region to be equipped with a directory terminal by the end of 1982.

The French PTT has said that these terminals will be given away free of charge. Their use, according to the PTT, should lead to cost savings in the long term. The PTT has calculated that equipping every subscriber in France with an electronic telephone directory will work out to be less expensive than continuing with the current printed directories and operator enquiry service (a phone-in enquiry service to human assistants will continue to operate, though on a much reduced scale).

To equip every telephone subscriber in France will require more than 30 million terminals. The French PTT expects to achieve this by the early 1990s. Table 11.2 shows its plan for annual terminal connections.

Table 11.2. Plan for installing electronic telephone directory terminals

	1980	1981	1982	1983	1984	1985	1986	1987	1988	1989	1990	1991	1992
Number of main telephone lines $\times 10^6$	16.0	17.9	19.8	21.6	23.3	25.0	26.4	27.9	29.2	30.5	31.8	32.5	33.3
Number of terminals $\times 10^6$	0	0.02	0.27	0.8	2.0	4.0	6.6	10	14	18	22	26	30

By 1979, the PTT had already placed a 'pre-series order' for 1000 terminals from each of four French suppliers: Matra, Thomson CSF, Telic and TRT Radiotechnique. Prototype terminals from each of these suppliers were demonstrated during 1979. The PTT's expectation was to select the best (or possibly the two best) during the preliminary trials in 1980, and then to place major production orders on all four suppliers.

All four prototypes featured small (about 7 inch) monochrome displays, with full alphanumeric keyboards. The terminals were designed to be very inexpensive. They had to meet the PTT's tender requirement of a unit price of 1000 French francs (about $250) for the first 100,000 units delivered. This was the price to the PTT. It excluded tax, and also an R&D element, which was paid separately by the PTT. With increasing production volumes, the PTT expected the unit price of a terminal to drop to around $100 by 1983. Before then, surplus production capacity should be available to permit terminal exports.

Because the electronic directory terminals use the Antiope standard, it will be possible also to use them for the Teletel service.* This is very significant because a terminal market for Teletel will not have to be created—the electronic directory terminals will be given away free of charge. The French appear to have found an application which justifies issuing free terminals on a very large scale; once in place, they could be used for many other applications. This way, the 'chicken and egg' problem referred to in Chapter 3 can be overcome.

Another extension of interactive videotex which was under discussion in 1979 was interworking with facsimile, for the so-called 'Telecopie Grand Public' service. It envisaged low cost facsimile transceivers being connected in users' homes via TV display terminals. For the facsimile transceivers to be produced at a price acceptable to the mass market, very large volume production was going to be required. To gauge the response of industry, the PTT issued invitations to tender for production quantities of half a million units around the end of 1978.

The French PTT and the CCETT must take full credit for the vision and enthusiasm with which they have proposed and developed their far-ranging videotex concepts. They are firmly convinced that videotex will become the rule rather than the exception in France during the 1980s, and that France will become a major exporter of new information systems.

WEST GERMANY'S BILDSCHIRMTEXT

Telecommunications and broadcasting environment

West Germany has an up-to-date and efficient telephone service, resulting from an extensive network modernization programme which dates back to the 1950s. West Germany also has the world's most advanced telex network, and ambitious plans for new telecommunications services including teletext, two-way cable TV, and satellite broadcasting.

There are some 20 million telephone subscribers in West Germany, growing by about 1.5 million per annum. There are also about 25 million TVs in use.

Broadcasting and telecommunications are becoming increasingly hard to distinguish, and nowhere is this more apparent than in West Germany. The advent of new information services is focusing increasing attention on this issue. It is being brought to a head by rapidly advancing plans in several areas—

---

* It will be possible in a technical sense, though there may be regulatory constraints.

including cable TV, teletext, online information retrieval services and videotex itself. The private publishing industry, which is strong and well established, has been conducting a vigourous fight against the PTT's telecommunications monopoly, and state control over television.

Radio and TV stations are not-for-profit public corporations established by legislation of the Lander (state governments). Programmes can only be provided by the station or network, and not by private organizations such as newspapers. This follows a Supreme Court decision in 1961 which ruled that only companies set up under the public law could provide programme material. Overall control, but not the authority to control programme content, is vested in the Lander.

The Federal Government has responsibility for freedom of the press since it is in the private industry sector. It is a constitutional obligation of the Ministry of the Interior to ensure that the press is not hindered in any way. This means the Minister may be obliged to ensure that the press participates in new media developments.

The private publishing sector has been interested in teletext, claiming that it is news publishing and therefore in its domain despite the Supreme Court's decision of 1961. The broadcasters, of course, do not agree. In any case they regard teletext as potentially complementary to existing broadcasting, with the emphasis on programme details and TV story synopsis. They do not regard teletext as news.

The private news sector recognizes that the PTT's videotex system can provide an equally viable (and in some ways superior) opportunity to enter the home screen publishing market. But the issue of videotex regulation is still a major concern. It is a question which must be answered by the courts. If it is judged to be broadcasting, then presumably regulation will be with the Lander; if a federally controllable service, it will be regulated on the basis of a commercial concern.

Both the press and the PTT would prefer federal regulation. The PTT would prefer it because it fears the Lander might hamper progress. The press would prefer it because it wants the system for itself—as a newspaper system rather than as a general information system. To help it realize its own case, the PTT has made a point of emphasizing Bildschirmtext's user-to-user message capability. This is to demonstrate that it is more than a mere information retrieval service.

Whether the PTT will retain control of its videotex in the long term, how videotex relates to broadcast teletext, and what role the private newspaper industry will play were issues which were still unresolved at the end of the 1970s.

The PTT's Bildschirmtext

The West German Bundespost (PTT) announced in April 1977 its contracts with the BPO for the supply of Prestel software and know-how. It demonstrated its virtually identical Bildschirmtext system at the Berlin Funkaustellung radio and TV exhibition that autumn. The demonstration was both a success in its own right, and favourably received compared with the experimental broadcast teletext service shown at the same time. As a result, the Bundespost decided to proceed with an experimental pilot trial.

Following the British experience, the pilot trial was not public. Starting in 1978, it was planned to run about two years. The prime purpose was to demonstrate the system, and to recruit the support of the TV and electronics industry and the independent information industry. Several hundred potential information providers were identified before the end of 1979.

A public market trial was due to begin at the start of 1980 involving 2000–3000 participants in the Dusseldorf area. The Dusseldorf site was selected by market research institutes appointed by the Bundespost. The same institutes were to be responsible for selecting a cross-section of users. The services to be made available were information retrieval, closed user groups and messages. A key purpose of the planned message service was to demonstrate that Bildschirmtext is not just broadcasting, but an integrated service of which messages are an important ingredient.

By early 1979, well over 100 information providers had agreed to participate. They included a large number of publishing companies, four of the largest direct mail order houses, department stores, and TV and electronics companies. Over three-quarters were press-related.

As in Britain, the PTT has been anxious to remain an independent carrier, avoiding influencing the information on the system. The plan was that working groups of representatives from the PTT, information providers and TV industries should be created, and later developed into boards of control.

Participants in the Dusseldorf market trial were to pay for their TV terminals, for telephone connection, and for priced pages. In addition there would be a service subscription—expected to be 5 DM (about $3) per month, to cover the cost of modem rental and connect-time. The page prices were to be set by the information providers, as in Britain. In setting their prices, information providers would take into account the Bundespost's charge of 3 or 4 DM per page per centre per annum, and a transmission charge of one pfennig per page. The Bundespost has said it will be responsible for user billing, crediting part of the revenue to the relevant information provider.

Two GEC 4082 computers were installed in Dusseldorf during 1979 to support the market trial. A second dual GEC 4082 installation was also undertaken during 1979 in Berlin. The purpose of the Berlin installation was to permit information providers to carry out their non-public testing and page maintenance. Later, the Berlin installation could be used to support more market trial participants, or even a limited public service. Meanwhile in 1979, the original Darmstadt pilot trial centre was being used for software development.

Extensive software modifications were being tested in readiness for the market trial and a later public service.

If the Bildschirmtext market trials prove successful, the Bundespost has said that it could launch a public service by 1982. The emphasis will be on the residential market, with a big publicity campaign to convince the public of Bildschirmtext's virtues. Both the information providers and the TV terminal manufacturers are looking for large scale residential use.

The plan envisages a number of Bildschirmtext centres across the nation. Information will be stored both at the Bildschirmtext centres, and on host computer databases. The network configuration is shown in Figure 11.2.

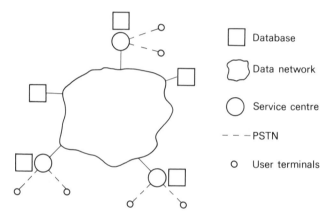

Figure 11.2. Bildschirmtext network schematic.

The tariff structure will be distance-independent, so that users wishing to access remote information are not penalized. Trunk lines in the network connecting Bildschirmtext centre with the host computers will use packet-switching at up to 48 kilobits per second. The first step in the software development program to support this concept, completed at the end of 1979, emulated the IBM 3270 terminal interface using a 7-level X25 protocol.

Although no ground rules had been set at the time of writing, it was likely that the big mail order houses and banks would prefer to use their own host computer databases rather than rent space from the Bundespost on its Bildschirmtext centres. Unlike the BPO, the Bundespost has been reluctant to make public predictions about the number of Bildschirmtext subscribers it expects to have in the future. But industry observers are confident that over a million will be reached before the end of the 1980s.

HOLLAND'S VIEWDATA*

Telecommunications and broadcasting environment

Holland's buoyant economy is reflected in its high telephone and TV penetration. With a population of 14 million and four and a half million households, it has over three million colour TVs installed and over four and a half million telephone connections. But the residential market for both colour TV and telephone connections is approaching saturation—with growth rates falling in both areas.

Holland's public voice telephone network is relatively modern and efficient. At the time of writing there were 800 switching centres, all of which were new or being modernized; over 100 were fully electronic. The others were sufficiently modern not to present problems with videotex. Sufficient spare capacity existed to support a gradually growing videotex service. The average spare capacity over peak time loads was 10%, though it was lower in towns than in rural areas.

There has been a considerable degree of regulatory concern about who in Holland should be responsible for videotex. This confusion has been partly due to the definition of the term broadcasting. Some government officials have regarded videotex as falling under broadcasting, defining it as a 'programme distributed by electronic transmission to an undifferentiated public'. The issue has been further complicated because commercial broadcasting is forbidden in Holland.

A national steering committee, with representatives from the ministries of Transportation, Culture and Recreation, Justice, Internal Affairs, Education and Science, was created in 1979 to 'accompany a public test service'. This must be seen as the first institutionalized attempt at governmental control of videotex. The issue which most occupied the committee at first was that of defining videotex as either a broadcasting or telephone activity. This was a political issue, and one which was not fully resolved by the end of 1979.

A resolution was expected either before or during the PTT's public market trial, expected to begin towards the end of 1980. Most observers expected that a separate law dealing with videotex would be enacted shortly afterwards.

Because of these uncertainties, the Dutch PTT's intention has been to develop both closed user group and publicly available services. Its interest in closed user group operations stemmed from an expectation that it was unlikely to be barred by law from offering such services itself.

PTT's Viewdata CUG and public service plans

Following careful studies and negotiations, the Dutch PTT announced in June 1978 that it had bought the rights to Prestel software and expertise from the BPO.

* Renamed Viditel in early 1980.

By September that year it was able to demonstrate its 'Viewdata' to visitors at the Firato radio and television exhibition in Amsterdam, using adapted TV terminals linked to a GEC computer in the Hague.

The demonstration was favourably received, both by the general public and by businessmen. On the basis of this positive response, the PTT formalized its plans to proceed. As a consequence of the deliberations of the national steering committee, it decided in 1979 to start a closed user group service for business subscribers, and to conduct a public market trial to form the basis of a full scale public service starting perhaps in late 1982 or early 1983.

The initial emphasis of the PTT's closed user group service will be on information retrieval. The PTT has also been studying ways of adding the capability to connect to external host computers (as with Bildschirmtext), for example for bookings and reservations.

Its closed user group proposal has met with an enthusiastic response. Those interested have included public libraries, real estate agents, government departments and legal, medical and travel firms.

The PTT envisages its closed user group operation developing into a service distinct from publicly available Viewdata. Custom tailoring will be essential to meet the demands for high system performance.

Despite the uncertainties surrounding a publicly available service, the PTT was still planning at the end of 1979 to conduct a one year public market trial of Viewdata beginning around the end of 1980. The trial was expected to aim at both residential and business participants, and to include comprehensive evaluations for the benefit of the service suppliers.

The policy of the PTT is to encourage a wide range of information providers in the same way as the BPO. It will be reluctant to limit the number of information providers participating, preferring to extend the database capacity if necessary. Around 200 potential information providers had shown keen interest before the end of 1979.

A total of about 4000 user participants is expected. Several hundred are expected to purchase their own terminals. A smaller number, probably 200–300, will be selected by the PTT on the basis of socio-demographical variables, and supplied with free terminals. Probably about 3000 participants will be identified by the information providers. And probably a few hundred participants will be sponsored by the TV industry itself.

The participants identified by the information providers should make up over half of the total. Each information provider is required to bring at least one participant into the trial for each allocation of fifty frames, as a condition of participation. The PTT feels that this is one way of overcoming the 'chicken and egg' problem apparent from the British experience.

The trial will be based on a dual GEC computer installation permitting twenty-four hour operation. The available capacity will be 200,000 frames, most of which are expected to be complete by the end of 1980. The responsibility for frame contents will lie with the information providers. The PTT, like the BPO, considers itself to be a neutral common carrier. However, for the market trial it will prevent information providers from offering information which it considers to be in any way controversial—for example, interpretable as either political, or invading privacy.

Having acquired a terminal, the expectation is that participants in the trial will pay additionally in four ways. These additional charges will be for telephone usage at regular rates, for connect-time to the Viewdata centre, for participation in the service through a subscription fee, and for retrieving information pages priced by the information providers.

Following the market trial, the PTT may proceed to a full scale public service, though there was no commitment at the end of 1979. The PTT's early plans for a public service envisaged the same kind of replicated database network as the BPO's proposal for its early Prestel public service. Later, however, the emphasis appeared to be more on the networked database approach proposed by the West Germans, permitting information providers to connect their databases stored on host computers directly into the network.

OTHER EUROPEAN COUNTRIES

Finland's Telset trials

Of the Nordic countries, only Finland appears to be free of bureaucratic or regulatory obstacles to rapid progress. Despite its proximity to Russia it is a haven of free enterprise. Telecommunications is virtually unregulated. Three-quarters of the two million telephone subscribers are served by private companies, of which there are over 60 altogether. The remaining subscribers are served by the PTT, which also supplies trunk routes.

The largest of the private telephone companies is Helsinki Telephone Company (HTC) which has over half a million telephones connected and about 150 telephone exchanges in the Helsinki area, serving a population of nearly a million.

There are about one and a half million TVs in Finland. About a quarter of a million colour TVs are installed in the Helsinki area.

HTC has been involved since the mid-1970s with a private videotex experiment called Telset. Telset started a year's trial in the summer of 1978. HTC has been involved with two other partners, Sanoma and Nokia. Encouraged by the success of the trial, the three partners have formed a jointly-owned subsidiary called Teletieto Oy.

Sanoma is the largest newspaper publisher in Finland, publishing the only national daily newspaper. Its interest in Telset is both as an information provider and a centre operator. It intends to lease out space to other information providers. Telset is both an investment for its cash resources and a protection for its future. In 1979 it anticipated no significant impact on its existing business for five to ten years.

Nokia is a diversified materials and equipment manufacturing group with about 10% of its turnover in electronics including terminals. Nokia does not make televisions, and its prime interest in Telset is in the business terminal market. About 30 terminals in total were attached to Telset during its early private trials. Half of these were business terminals—adaptations of standard Nokia unintelligent VDUs. The other half were adapted domestic TVs supplied by Sanoma.

The Telset trial continued until the end of 1979. The aim was to provide answers to a number of technical and marketing questions with a view to developing a Telset centre able to support around 200 simultaneous users. This was thought to be about the right size for a population of around 10,000 users. The Telset designers expected a nationwide service to require a network of regional and local centres. Conceivably a public service along these lines could begin in 1980.

Telset has been based on the Prestel concept. It features a display format of 40 characters per row and 24 rows per page, a character set including upper and lower case characters and symbols (identical to the Finnish data transmission code), 1200/75 bits per second duplex transmission, six colours in addition to black and white, and flashing and alphamosaic graphics. The Telset trials have been run on a DEC computer installed at Sanoma's headquarters in Helsinki. Special software has been written to run under the computer's operating system. The database is structured along broadly similar lines to Prestel's. At the start of the trial, information retrieval was the only application offered. But planning was already well advanced to extend Telset's services to include messages and computation in readiness for a public service, should it go ahead.

The Finnish PTT appeared to show little interest in Telset during its pilot trial. At that time it seemed unlikely that the PTT would develop its own system or intervene in the Telset enterprise.

Switzerland's Videotex

Following the announcement of its purchase of Prestel software and knowhow from the BPO in the spring of 1979, the Swiss PTT made plans to begin a pilot trial before the end of the year. A public market trial of the system, named Videotex, was planned to begin in 1980.

The Swiss PTT contracted with Standard Telephone and Radio (STR), a Swiss subsidiary of ITT, to establish the Videotex pilot trial centre. STR's responsibility included the installation of a GEC 4082 computer, together with responsibility for modifying the Prestel software to match Swiss requirements.

By the summer of 1979, SVIPA, the Swiss Videotex Information Providers Association, had been established with 21 members. The information providers represented a variety of industry sectors including travel, mail order, publishing, manufacturing and financial. The plan was for the pilot trial to be restricted to the information providers, the PTT and a select group of businesses.

The Swiss PTT was expecting to contract for the public market trial hardware and software during 1980. The intention was for it to be extended with a public service later on. There was no commitment to Prestel or to GEC beyond the pilot trial.

Assuming satisfactory results from the market trial, a full public service could begin as early as 1982, although 1983 seems a more likely date.

Sweden's DataVision

The Swedish PTT, Televerket, has a monopoly of all the transmission facilities in Sweden. However, this is not a legal monopoly—there are no rules to limit it. The telephone service is good, with a penetration of around 90% of households. Call charges are generally low, local calls being free.

When the videotex concept first emerged, the Swedish newspapers lobbied for and got a government commission. Its brief was to look at teletext, videotex and facsimile, and to recommend who should run and regulate which, whether advertisements should be permitted, and what the likely effect might be on the press. An interim report was issued towards the end of 1979 with the full report due to follow in 1980.

While the government commission continued to debate the ramifications of videotex, the PTT was already conducting experiments with its own DataVision system. During 1976 and 1977, the PTT had been able to gain valuable experience with Britain's Prestel. But it decided against buying the Prestel software. Instead it developed its own software to run on a Data General Nova computer installed in Stockholm in late 1977.

A private pilot trial of DataVision started early in 1979. Only a limited number of information providers participated in this trial, mostly from the publishing industry. Other fields represented included weather forecasting, banking, international trade and pharmaceuticals. Each information provider was allocated about one hundred frames and given free use of editing terminals.

At the time of the pilot trial, DataVision shared Prestel's display and transmission standards and, like Prestel, it offered database searching through numbered menu choices. However, the intention was for the software to be enhanced with keyword searching, calculation and message services. These enhancements were to be implemented during 1980.

Depending on the result of the government commission's investigation, the PTT could start a public market trial in 1980 or 1981 with up to 1000 users. A public service might develop from this, possibly by 1983.

The PTT appears to have harboured some doubts about the readiness of the residential marketplace to adopt its DataVision in the short term, mainly for price reasons. If a public service does go ahead, it is likely to be aimed at first at the business community.

Other national plans

Several other European countries have been following videotex developments closely, though they had made no formal announcements about their own plans before the end of 1979.

Austria will be strongly influenced by developments in West Germany. In early 1979 it appeared quite likely that the Austrian PTT would negotiate with the BPO for Prestel software and know-how. By the end of the year, an agreement involving the Bundespost seemed a likely possibility.

In *Belgium*, teletext was creating more interest at the end of the 1970s than videotex. The two radio and TV broadcasting companies (RTB and BRT, French and Flemish respectively) were both actively investigating teletext systems. But because the broadcasters banned participation by publishers in teletext, there has been a strong interest amongst publishers in videotex.

In *Denmark*, a government committee was established in 1979 along similar lines to Sweden's, charged with the responsibility of examining the social and political implications of videotex. At the end of 1979 the Danish PTT was continuing to show interest in the potential of videotex as a revenue source, and seemed likely to proceed with plans to start a two year public market trial some time in 1981. A number of private sector information providers, especially newspapers, have shown strong support for videotex.

The PTT was still uncommitted to a specific system, and it appeared possible that Danish industry would develop its own videotex system.

In *Italy* representatives from industry and from the PTT have attended a number of meetings and demonstrations of videotex. But no public commitment had been made by the end of 1979.

In *Norway*, the PTT has tried to interest local industry in a pilot service, but the start date has continually slipped. As in Sweden, a state commission has been dabating the future of information media on a broad front. But at the end of 1979 it did seem likely that the PTT would start a pilot trial of videotex in 1980 with a view to conducting a public market trial later. One of the PTT's plans was to make 10,000 information pages available in the market trial to about a hundred selected users. Information providers thought likely to participate in the trial included newspapers and publishing concerns, banks, the Norwegian consumer association, and travel organizations including SAS.

In *Spain*, research into videotex has been spurred by FUNDESCO, a not-for-profit communications research organization controlled by the Spanish PTT. Towards the end of 1979, the Spanish PTT was able to demonstrate a privately developed videotex system, though it was still continuing to negotiate with other suppliers for software and knowhow. At that time it appeared possible that Spain would wish to start a pilot trial in 1980, though there was an increasing desire to await the outcome of the standardization debate.

PRIVATE AND CLOSED USER GROUP SYSTEMS

Services in Britain

The Prestel publicity in Britain and the BPO's endeavours to attract business interest have encouraged many private companies to consider the alternative of in-house videotex systems. A few had already implemented in-house services by 1979, and many others were in the active planning stage. The systems could be home grown or purchased off the shelf.

Three companies had already announced videotex systems for sale to support in-house services before the end of 1979: GEC, Philips and Thorn-ICL. The system configurations offered ranged from single station intelligent editing terminals through to multiple port computers and software able to support several hundred terminals, with capacities of tens of thousands of information pages.

Whitbread Limited, the London based multi-million dollar food and beverage company, was the first to announce publicly its use of an in-house videotex system, called DAISY, which it developed itself.

By the end of 1979, Whitbread had accumulated around two years' experience with up to 12 Prestel terminals—mostly coloured—attached to a dedicated Data General Nova minicomputer. The main application was stock control information for storeroom clerks and senior managers. The database size was over 8000 information frames, updated daily by re-loading from the company's Honeywell mainframe. The software was specially written for the application, using interfaces to the Prestel standard.

The reaction from users appears to have been very positive. They have said they like the colour, and easy system accessibility. The colour has helped improve the readibility of columns of figures, permitting more data to be displayed on a frame than otherwise. Compared with the alternative of conventional VDUs attached to the mainframe, Whitbread has not claimed that DAISY has saved money. But ease of use, not cost saving, was the objective—an objective which Whitbread claims to have achieved.

A second British in-house videotex service is the Stock Exchange's Topic, again developed internally specifically for the purpose. Topic's aim is to provide subscribers in London and the provinces with up-to-the-second information on stock market prices and news. Topic was planned to become operational in May 1980, with 400 terminals connected by the end of the year. Clients had already placed advanced orders for 500 terminals by the end of 1979. The system was expected to grow rapidly to 2000 terminals and beyond.

Topic has been designed to replace the Stock Exchange's MPDS (Market Price Display System). MPDS was first installed in 1968 using regular monochrome TVs as display terminals. By the end of the 1970s over 2000 terminals were connected to a 22 channel cable. Users could select any one of the channels at a time to display the frame of information currently being transmitted on that channel using full video bandwidth. MPDS has proved to be reliable and inexpensive. It has also been able to offer instantaneous response. But the limited number of channels available meant a severe limitation on the amount of information which could be displayed. Moreover the use of cable has limited the opportunities for connecting new subscribers, particularly outside London.

Topic has been designed to offer superior features and flexibility at similar cost levels to MPDS. Its design goals have led to some interesting features. A number of minicomputers (Modcomp Classic), one initially and one standby, will support about 1000 terminals each. Each minicomputer is expected to handle a peak traffic load of 200 information page requests per second whilst maintaining a response time of less than a second.

The terminals are designed to be connected in clusters of eight or more per port—each cluster attached to a sub-multiplexor. The port-to-sub-multiplexor connections are planned to run at 9600 bits per second.

The basic transmission code, character set and interface standards are all Prestel compatible. But the Stock Exchange's specification for Topic terminals features programmable micro control to permit each terminal to be adapted to alternative standards. The specification calls for a raster which is non-interlaced to reduce flicker, though at the expense of resolution. At 9600 bits per second, the screen fill time should be less than a second.

Other British companies which were planning in-house videotex systems at the time of writing included a major automobile manufacturer, a diversified food and leisure industry group, a major industrial equipment supplier, a major British subsidiary of an established US confectionary business, and a major retail department store chain. An important attraction was synergy: their terminals could be used for the in-house system, and for publicly available Prestel and other closed user group services. The potential ubiquity of the Prestel interface was compelling.

Private services in Holland

In Holland, the PTT has acknowledged that several videotex networks can exist side by side. The PTT issues specifications regarding the use of the public telephone network, but cannot enter into the question of the contents of data traffic. This means in practice that provided they comply with technical rules and pose no threats to regular telephone traffic, private network operators can offer their own videotex services.

Verenigde Nederlandse Uitgeversbedrijven (VNU) was the first commercial enterprise to operate a private videotex network. VNU is the largest publishing group in Holland with an annual turnover exceeding 1 billion guilders (half a billion dollars). VNU has interests in newspapers, books and encyclopaedias, magazines, the graphic industry and computer software development. Traditionally it has focused primarily on the Dutch language market, but towards the end of the 1970s it adopted a strategy of internationalizing its operation.

VNU's belief that career data would be a viable videotex operation led to the creation of TVS (Toegepaste Viewdata Systemen) in early 1979. TVS was conceived to develop *Jobdata*, originally the product of VNU's subsidiary Intermediair. Intermediair issues a controlled circulation weekly containing personnel advertisements, which is distributed to over 100,000 graduates.

Following an agreement with Insac, TVS obtained the exclusive marketing rights to the Prestel software in Holland. By mid-1979, TVS had announced its plan to open a videotex service bureau to closed group users. Located in the VNU main computer centre, the service included rental or sale of terminals, the provision of communications facilities and the development of application software.

TVS's videotex service bureau was equipped with a single GEC 4082 computer in June 1979. The initial configuration was 32 ports and a page capacity of 140,000.

TVS's aim has been to create a large user population as quickly as possible. Its strategy has been to permit access to its information to anyone with a compatible videotex terminal (i.e. Prestel terminal) and authorization to access the database. Participants in the PTT's Viewdata market trial, for example, could obtain access.

Although no agreements had been concluded by the end of 1979, VNU's negotiations were at an advanced stage with a number of organizations for setting up closed user group Jobdata services, and with other business associations supplying real estate, travel and medical information.

CHAPTER 12

DEVELOPMENTS IN THE USA

THE REGULATORY ENVIRONMENT

Telecommunications, AT&T, and the role of the FCC

The US telephone service is characterized by private companies competing for market shares. This is in sharp contrast to the monopolistic privileges enjoyed by the PTTs in Europe. But two key factors colour the picture in the USA. The first is the regulatory control of the FCC. The second is the dominant position of AT&T (American Telephone and Telegraph which, together with its 23 operating companies, Bell Labs and Western Electric, is known collectively as the *Bell System*).

Regulation is a way of introducing control over private businesses in lieu of competition—where such competition, if unrestricted, might be inefficient or counter to the public interest. Regulation of US interstate telephone services began in 1910 under the Interstate Commerce Commission. It remained superficial until responsibility was assumed by the FCC (Federal Communications Commission) under the Communications Act of 1934. Intrastate Commissions were formed in the decade commencing in 1910.

The FCC is an independent agency whose scope is defined by enabling legislation. Hence it is interpretable by the courts. Its seven Commissioners, appointed by the President and approved by the Senate, serve overlapping terms. Its responsibilities include entry and exit conditions for industry participants, service permissibility, and allowable rates of return on investment for participants.

In the US today the communications carriers run a $50 billion business. Over 80% of the revenue accrues to AT&T, which has a near monopoly over Interstate Telephone Services, and over 80% of the 170-odd million telephones installed. The remainder is shared by around 1600 independent companies. The largest of these independents is GTE. Although its revenues are only about 10% of AT&T's, it is close to the BPO in terms of numbers of telephones installed.

Since 1968, AT&T's monopolistic position has come under increasing threat. The change has been in favour of the independents, many of whom have been able both to prosper and to grow. AT&T is now having to work hard against increasing competition in every quarter.

The change began following the 1968 FCC decision permitting a small company—Carterfone—to attach devices directly to the telephone network. The Carterfone decision opened the door to independents to design, make and market devices for attachment. At first these had to be via AT&T supplied PCAs (Protective Connecting Arrangements). Later they could be attached directly. Now all that is needed prior to connection is device registration with the FCC demonstrating conformity to standards.

Following the Carterfone decision, a further change permitted specialized carriers to compete against AT&T's monopoly of the provision of interstate private line circuits for both voice and data. This resulted firstly from the challenge of MCI, which introduced a competing switched long distance service over the opposition of both AT&T and the FCC. The challenge was upheld by the courts on the grounds that the FCC had never made a proper administrative ruling that the public switched telephone network was a telephone company monopoly in the public interest.

A second reason for the change was the FCC's approval of 'resale' services. The independents were permitted to lease interstate private lines from AT&T, and to resell the capacity to third-party users in the form of *value added* services. By arranging efficient use of the wires through capacity sharing techniques, the value added carriers (like Tymnet) could offer commercially attractive rates.

AT&T has been fighting back over the independents' threat to its long haul (interstate) business on the grounds of the need to preserve its 'system integrity'. The independents have alleged that AT&T cross-subsidizes its local intrastate operations from profits accrued on the lucrative interstate services. However, tentative agreements on fund contributions from long distance services to local companies were reached by the end of the 1970s. The intention was that they should form a framework within which both AT&T and the independent companies could operate.

Finally, the *open skies* policy introduced during the Nixon administration further threatens AT&T's position in the future. The policy permits independents to offer unrestricted domestic communications by satellite. As the cost of satellite links continues to fall, the impact of this new medium will become increasingly strongly felt.

Videotex and regulation

Telecommunications is federally regulated through the FCC and the underlying Communications Act of 1934. Data processing has been deemed to lie in the private sector domain, and is unregulated. However, in recent years data processing has become increasingly intertwined with communications. More and more computer users are linked to computers from remote locations using communication lines. And the technology of communications has itself become increasingly dependent on computing techniques, following the rapid advent of digital telecommunications techniques. To use the somewhat hackneyed catchphrase of the 1970s, computing and telecommunications are converging.

The problem confronting the FCC in its regulatory role has been a definitional one: to draw clear boundaries between computing and telecommunications in order to define the territory in which the two sectors may operate. It has been trying to defend the indefensible—to establish a distinction between computing and communications that increasingly does not exist.

Where does videotex stand? The answer in 1979 was still somewhat ambiguous. This was because videotex can provide more than one type of service. As an information retrieval service, the position was fairly clear. As a message service, this was not the case.

If an operator were to provide the computer system with database storage, as the BPO does for Prestel, there is ample precedent in current information and timesharing services for videotex to be construed as data processing and not communications. Hence it would not be subject to regulation. An unregulated operator would merely be left with the risks of the free market and potential problems of standardization with which to contend.

If a communications carrier other than AT&T were to offer such a service, it would be required under the FCC's maximum separation policy to offer it through a separate corporation. Since a number of carriers have already done just this for data processing services, this is not an obstacle of consequence.

AT&T alone does not have the latter alternative due to the 1956 Consent Decree, and is therefore presently barred from offering such a service. However, this no longer appears to be a permanent proscription. There is mounting pressure to find a way of removing this restriction on AT&T whilst also deregulating non-monopoly areas.* Another possibility for AT&T, under current regulation alternatives, is to provide a videotex system up to but excluding the databases themselves. AT&T would complete the connection between a user and the requested database, and then do no more than communications processing on the information flow between the two.

Message communications services, however, are a breed whose status is less clear. In terms of regulated communications services, the FCC 'has endorsed an open entry policy with respect to most types of domestic record communication services, the principal exception being public message telegraph services'. Even

---

* The regulatory environment governing telecommunications services is under review, and could change significantly as a consequence of the Second Computer Inquiry.

that exception has been under enquiry. Open entry private record communication services are 'characterized by the requirement for private subscription to the service before use and by the condition that the originator of the message be a subscriber'. Should a viewdata service be offered which is dominantly message communications, it appears it would fit comfortably in the private open entry category.

PROLIFERATING PRIVATE SECTOR PLANS

The videotex scene in the US is characterized by a proliferating number of trials and service plans. Some are aiming at the business marketplace; others at the residential marketplace. Equipment, standards and information services are different and fluid. The early years of the 1980s will undoubtedly see increasing experimental activity, and probably major commercial developments as well.

AT&T's electronic information service (EIS)

AT&T began a six month test of its EIS videotex system among users in the Albany, New York area in August 1979. The test users were provided with a visual display terminal with an alphanumeric keyboard free of charge.

In addition to area code 518 white and yellow pages, the EIS database offered users the Manhattan yellow pages, news and sports headlines, weather, horoscopes and advice. All these services were similar to those already widely available through the telephone. In AT&T's view, EIS did not represent a trespass into a non-telecommunications domain.

During the EIS trial, fifteen TEC 570 terminals were rotated among the users at two-week intervals. When the test was finished, EIS had entered well over a hundred homes. The plan was for test participants to be interviewed to determine their response, and to question what kind of services they would like to see on the system.

Albany was chosen because of its representative population cross-section, and the availability of computerized directory records which AT&T operators have long been using.

AT&T's interest in videotex is unlikely to finish with the trial period. It is known to be interested in the potential of TV as an information terminal. AT&T is also involved in the Knight-Ridder Viewtron trial in Florida described below.

GTE's Viewdata

GTE is second in size only to AT&T, with interests in electronics and TV manufacture through its Sylvania Entertainment Products Division.

During 1979, GTE began testing a version of Prestel in the USA. In June 1979, GTE announced that it had negotiated exclusive rights to Prestel in the North American market for an undisclosed sum. This followed prolonged negotiations with Insac Inc. (the US subsidiary of Insac, the British company formed in 1977 with state money provided through the National Enterprise Board to market British software and knowhow overseas) during the latter half of 1978 and early 1979.

About the end of 1979, GTE announced that it had signed contracts with over 20 major US companies. Among them were Chase Manhattan Bank, J. Walter Thompson Advertising Agency, publishers McGraw-Hill and Time, and stockbrokers Merrill Lynch. These customers were expected to link to the GTE Computer Center in Tampa, Florida, via GTE's Telenet packet-switching network. If the tests proved successful, GTE was expected to expand the service into the residential marketplace with its customers providing information.

Insac's Viewdata

The contract which Insac Inc. negotiated with GTE provided GTE with exclusive rights to use Prestel in the mass business and consumer marketplaces. Insac Inc. itself retained the right to offer Prestel for corporate internal communications, and for closed user group applications.

During 1979, Insac proceeded with its plan to establish its own Viewdata service. It obtained signed letters of intent from GIANTS—an association of 450 Travel Agents—and with the Peoria Journal Star, a large newspaper, magazine and radio station in central Illinois. These letters of intent were preliminary to Insac's own plan to sell terminals and port access to its own videotex computer in the USA.

Also during 1979, Insac began the task of re-writing Prestel in FORTRAN to run on DEC PDP-11 computers. The modified version of Prestel was designed to run with terminals having full alphanumeric keyboards. The display grid was also enlarged beyond Prestel's original 40 × 24.

Knight-Ridder's Viewtron

Knight-Ridder is a one-billion dollar newspaper company headquartered in Florida, with additional interests in radio and TV. It prints and distributes three and a half million newspapers daily from 22 locations in the USA.

In April 1979, Knight-Ridder announced the formation of a wholly owned subsidiary called Viewdata Corporation of America Inc. (VCA) with the purpose of developing and testing a videotex service called Viewtron. The service was to use modified TVs connected by a telephone line to a central computer owned and operated by VCA. A budget of $1.3 million was earmarked for spending in the following two years.

Knight-Ridder's announced plan for Viewtron has taken the form of a six month market trial to start in April 1980 in 150–200 homes in the Coral Gables, Florida area. Coral Gables is an enclave city within Miami. According to Knight-Ridder, it was selected because of its population of 'mobile, affluent, educated inhabitants, who have a sense of group identity coupled with catholic information needs'.

Thirty adapted TVs were to be rotated among the user participants. They were to be based on RCA colour TVs modified to a Bell design with integral decoders, and built by Western Electric. The plan was for the terminals to use a display grid of 40 × 20. The transmission and display standard would be specially developed, and would feature DRCS (dynamically redefinable character sets).

Viewtron was expected to offer the test participants a wide choice of information including news, weather, sports results, movie schedules, feature stories, consumer product ratings and a variety of reference information on topics such as boating and fishing. By the end of 1979, 22 separate information-providing organizations had helped to prepare 4000 frames of information on the system. The information providers included the Congressional Quarterly, the Associated Press, Macmillan Publishing Company, Addison-Wesley Publishing Company and the Miami Herald, Knight-Ridder's flagship newspaper.

VCR was also planning to test advertising applications. The test users would receive both classified and display advertising. At the end of 1979, some 15 organizations had been identified who were prepared to advertise on Viewtron, including Eastern Airlines, AAA Worldwide Travel Agency, Grand Union, J C Penney, Shell Oil, and B Dalton Booksellers.

Apart from its responsibility for designing and building adapted TV terminals, AT&T was reported to be joining with Knight-Ridder in the Viewtron trial in order to gain detailed insights about consumer acceptance.

Ohio College Library Center's (OCLC's) Channel 2000

OCLC is a $30 million not-for-profit organization based in Columbus, Ohio, which operates a national computer network for libraries. One of the world's largest online service providers, the OCLC catalogue contained five and a half million entries in 1979, to which were attached nearly 50 million location listings.

About the end of 1979, OCLC announced its 'Channel 2000' videotex experiment, to be conducted among some 200 home users in the Columbus metropolitan area towards the end of 1980. Banc One, an innovative local bank, is a partner in the project.

At the time of Channel 2000's announcement, the plan was for information on the test database to include extracts from OCLC's computer file of Columbus library catalogues, encyclopaedic topics provided by the American Academic Encyclopaedia of Princeton New Jersey, and banking information from Banc One's records (available only to the bank's customers, of course).

Channel 2000 will be free of charge to the selected participants. Most of the participants were to be provided with external adaptors for their existing TVs, the adaptors featuring acoustic modems (300 bits per second), with either numeric-only or alphanumeric keyboards, and TV attachment through the antenna socket. In addition, a few purpose-designed, compact, monochrome terminals were to be supplied, in order to test the public reaction.

At the time of Channel 2000's announcement, OCLC had no commitment to a service beyond that particular experiment.

Other telephone based experiments

Apart from those described above, a number of other experiments were being planned, or were already underway, during 1979. Some of them are described below.

RCA was examining videotex's market potential in a series of carefully designed tests. It started with a limited programme of demonstrations in New England using TV terminals supplied by Insac, and connected to the Prestel database in London. Further tests followed, aimed at exploring in more detail the response of consumers to videotex.

Compuserve, a $15 million timesharing company based in Columbus, Ohio, started to offer its MicroNET videotex-like service in 1979. MicroNet allowed owners of personal computers to access the storage of Compuserve's mainframe computers by making a local telephone call. Subscribers were able to pay a subscription charge of $9, together with an access fee of $5 per hour during off-peak times—6 pm to 5 am on weekdays, plus weekends. In addition, subscribers paid their local telephone charge.

The main emphasis of Compuserve was on software distribution, with users able to access the MicroNET program library. In addition, personal file storage and user-to-user electronic mail was provided. A wide range of programs was available for downloading from the library including games, text editing, utilities, mathematics and statistics.

By the end of 1979 Compuserve's plans for the future included the provision of information such as news, weather, stock quotations, details of commodity options and encyclopaedic information.

Another important development announced during 1979 was the *Source*. The Source was announced by TCA, the Telecomputing Corporation of America, a subsidiary of Digital Broadcasting Corporation of McLean, Virginia. The Source was presented as offering some 2000 programs to home computer users. They included income tax preparation, text editing, games, a store and forward electronic mail package, and also the UPI newswire service.

The Source's pricing strategy included a $100 subscription fee, and a charge of $2.75 per hour inclusive for connection to the database. The low connect-time charge resulted from the Source's use of the Telenet packet-switching service at off-peak times between 6 pm and 7 am on weekdays and all weekends. Local connection to Telenet is toll free; Telenet had ports in over 200 US cities in 1979.

Another two-way telephone videotex service aimed at home computer users during 1979 was *Dow Jones'* experimental programme for users of Apple II home computers. It began in April, offering news and financial information to six Texas families in Los Colinas, a residential and commercial development located between Dallas and Fort Worth. The six families, along with two businesses also involved in the experiment, were able to gain instant access to Dow Jones' news and stock quotations using their Apple II computer terminals, a television receiver and a typewriter-like printer. The information was transmitted from Dow Jones' central computer at South Brunswick, New Jersey, using a combination of land telephone lines and local cable.

Although the trial was originally scheduled to last only three months, it was extended indefinitely in mid-1979. The plan was to increase the number of terminal users to a minimum of 25. The purpose was to collect more data from more people about information needs and usage.

An experiment typifying how a specialist market might develop is the US Department of Agriculture's (USDA's) *Green Thumb* experiment aimed at farmers. Green Thumb is a joint venture between USDA, The National Weather Service, and the University of Kentucky. The plan has been to transmit farming information, including data on crops, weather and commodity prices, to some 200 farmers in the Kentucky counties of Todd and Shelby beginning in 1980. If successful, the experiment was going to be extended to farmers in other Kentucky counties, and then to other States.

The database was to be stored in microcomputers in County Government offices for transmission over telephone lines using modems supplied by South Central Bell. The microcomputers were to be updated from information held in Central State computers.

The Green Thumb concept is interesting because it relies on a 'dump and disconnect' mode of operation. Farmers participating in the experiment will attach Green Thumb boxes between the regular telephone and the TV via its antenna socket. Each Green Thumb box will contain sufficient local memory to store a complete videotex magazine of eight pages of information.

Each magazine will be transmitted in just a few seconds. A farmer will use his keypad attached to the Green Thumb box to extract the pages of information from the stored magazine one at a time for display on the TV. The advantage of this mode of operation, which has the appearance of being one-way in nature, is that it reduces both telephone and port occupancy times.

The Green Thumb terminal display grid is 16×32. In late 1979 it was announced that the decoder equipment in the Green Thumb boxes was to be made by Motorola, the assembly of the boxes being subcontracted to Tandy Corporation, the well-established manufacturers of personal computers.

Two-way cable TV experience

An alternative medium to the telephone for distributing videotex to users is cable. By 1979, the number of households receiving CATV* through a cable rather than through the air reached 15 million—20% of all TV owning households in the USA. Over 200,000 miles of cable have been laid during the past 20 years. After a hesitant start, it has become a booming business. The top 50 cable operators alone have been planning to lay another 40,000 miles of cable during 1980 alone.

But virtually all the cable laid to date has been one-way only. Interactive videotex requires a two-way connection, as with the telephone. For videotex, a reverse channel is needed to transmit back from the TV. In recent years there has been an increasing amount of interest by the cable operators both in the potential of one-way-only teletext information systems, and two-way videotex. But two-way cable is more expensive than one-way. And converting existing one-way cable is particularly expensive; it means inserting special amplifiers at frequent intervals along a cable. Although all new cable systems laid in the USA since 1972—about 70% of the total—are designed to be upgraded to two-way, a very average figure in 1979 for the cost of conversion was around $200 per subscriber for a typical medium sized urban installation.

In a sense, though, using cable is an ideal way to bring videotex to the residential market. Televisions are already connected, and there is no need to interfere with the telephone. The cable operators are established, and are serving defined communities. Customer contact and billing mechanisms are in place. At first sight, videotex systems could readily be established at many transmitting head-ends.

The problem is that the cable operators are not wholly convinced of the market need for videotex, and are already busy responding to the existing demand for their services. Cable TV subscribers are people who want to watch more, or clearer, TV than they get over the air. Cable offers a solution to air

* Cable TV is often abbreviated to CATV. Strictly speaking, this stands for Community Antenna TV, reflecting the nature of the service when it first appeared.

broadcasting's problem of transmission interference from large obstacles like hills and tall buildings. And although three-quarters of the existing cable is limited to about 12 simultaneous channels, many of the newer cables have a capacity two or three times as great. For these benefits, subscribers typically pay around $10 per month. The habit has been growing rapidly. The average annual growth rate of the cable TV industry exceeded 20% per year in the last two years of the 1970s.

Faced with a growing demand for their traditional services, it is hardly surprising that cable TV operators are reticent about developing wholly new services. Nonetheless, at least a few have been actively exploring the potential of videotex. It is highly probable that the early 1980s will see at least some cable operators experimenting with videotex services.

One two-way cable service had already achieved a great deal of publicity before the end of the 1970s. This was Warner Communication's Qube Service in Columbus, Ohio. At that time, Qube was reaching around 30,000 subscribers. But Qube is not videotex. The purpose of its two-way feature is to permit users to interact with current TV shows such as auctions, quiz shows, panel discussions and games. Although it had been somewhat disdainful about videotex at times, Warner nonetheless hinted at plans to incorporate a videotex capability in future Qube experiments.

CHAPTER 13

DEVELOPMENTS IN CANADA

THE REGULATORY ENVIRONMENT

The private operators and regulation

Regulation of telecommunications carriers in Canada is split between federal and provincial jurisdiction. Of the major carriers, Bell Canada (Ontario and Quebec), British Columbia Telephones (British Columbia) and CN/CP Telecommunications are federally regulated, and the remaining carriers are provincially regulated. The federal carriers are restricted to carriage and are impeded from being in the content business. Federally regulated carriers are restricted in their involvement in the data processing business unless it is undertaken via 'arms length' subsidiaries. Some provincially regulated carriers, however, can be involved directly in the data processing business.

Cable penetration in Canada far exceeds that of the USA. Over 50% of Canadian households have a cable service, and cable plant passes by approximately 70% of all households. Broadcasting, including the cable TV industry, falls under federal regulatory control. The prime purpose of regulation in this area is cultural protection and, more specifically, the protection of the Canadian broadcasting system. Thus it is unlikely that the cable television industry will be free of content restrictions with the introduction of new services. The Department of Communications (DoC) is responsible for the regulation of technical specifications related to broadcasting undertakings.

The connection of data devices to the public switched telephone network is more restrictive in Canada than in the US, due to the telephone company practices. Except for a limited number of certified devices such as telephone answering machines, an attachment must be made either with an acoustic coupler or via a data connector with any type of modem, or via a telephone company supplied modem.

Department of Communications' Telidon

The Department of Communications (DoC) Research Centre has developed its own videotex system called Telidon. Telidon has created worldwide interest. It was first demonstrated publicly in Europe during 1979, when its high display resolution gained a great deal of attention and an enthusiastic response. The DoC has had no plans to implement a Telidon service itself, but Telidon technology will be employed, with the assistance of the DoC, in a number of Canadian videotex trials which are described below.

Telidon can be thought of as a videotex standard, in the same way as Antiope. The key characteristic of Telidon is independence between the information stored at the database, and the terminal display. The goal is to ensure that changes in terminal design (particularly resolution) do not jeopardize the usefulness of databases which have already been painstakingly and expensively established.

Graphical data can be stored on the database in the form of drawing commands, using picture description instructions (PDIs). Any terminal able to decode the PDIs can present a display. The display resolution becomes a function of the terminal's resolution capability, and not of the data. This opens the door to future changes to TV resolution without jeopardizing the database.

Using the drawing commands, a frame designer can, for example, draw a cube on the screen of a data entry terminal and then increase or decrease its size using simple key commands, or a light pen. The DoC has insisted that frame creation and editing takes no longer with Telidon than with Prestel or Antiope, though it does mean using a special purpose intelligent editing terminal.

The use of drawing commands enables complex shapes to be defined and displayed without having to transmit voluminous information. During 1979, the DoC was able to demonstrate Telidon terminals connected at 1200 bits per second, and able to construct full frame displays in about the same time as the average for Prestel or Antiope, i.e. around 5 seconds. The alphageometric displays on these Telidon terminals were not up to the full video quality of a TV picture, though, because they were restricted by internal memory capacity. More expensive terminals, with more memory capacity, could display higher resolution graphics from the same transmitted information.

Apart from drawing commands, Telidon also permits encoded text to be transmitted. Thus Telidon terminals can display alphanumerics, and have been demonstrated handling multiple language character sets.

Finally Telidon has an alphaphotographic capability. Information which cannot be coded either in alphanumeric or alphageometric form can be transmitted as a bit stream (as in facsimile) for reconstruction on a terminal display.

153

PROLIFERATING PLANS FOR TELIDON VIDEOTEX

By the end of 1979, several videotex trials using Telidon were planned or already under way.

Alberta General Telephone's (AGT's) Vidon

Alberta General Telephone was planning to start its own field trial of the Telidon system in the summer of 1980. A 10,000 page database was planned, with terminals distributed among 120 residential users in the Calgary area. Apart from Telidon videotex, additional services were also going to be tested, including emergency monitoring and energy management.

Bell Canada's Vista

Bell Canada was due to start a twelve month market trial of its Vista videotex system in early 1981, following a pilot trial with 25 terminals during 1979 conducted by Bell Northern Research.

Twenty-five alphamosaic type terminals were used during the pilot trial, connected to a database with 3500 frames of information on a DEC computer in Ottawa. The information was created and maintained by two of Canada's largest newspaper publishers—Torstar Corporation and Southam Inc. Both information retrieval and message services were demonstrated.

Following the pilot trial, the market trial was expected to involve around 1000 terminals, all of which would be to the Telidon standard. Most of the participants were to be drawn from the residential community, though some business participants were to be included as well. Closed user groups were also likely to be involved with representatives from the real estate, travel, education and government sectors.

Around 75,000 pages of information were planned from about 30 information providers including Torstar and Southam. The database topics were expected to include travel, news, weather, sports headlines, consumer bulletins, entertainment details, directories, classified advertising, and stock quotations. Both English and French languages were to be tested. It was also possible that a message service would be included; teleshopping and airline reservations were likely applications. The first phase of the trial was expected to run for 12 months, with no user charges during the period.

Probably all the user terminals in the trial will be fitted with numeric-only keypads. The terminals will be designed by Bell Northern Research and manufactured by Northern Telecoms, and possibly by Norpak also. The terminals will be able to display high quality graphics, many of which will be prepared directly from photographs.

The computer will be a DEC PDP-11 with 64 dial-up ports on loan from the DoC, and with DoC software. If a message service is featured, it is likely to be supported by a separate computer.

Assuming a satisfactory response, the Vista trial will be extended to a second phase to evaluate pricing strategies and billing and payment mechanisms. If this works out satisfactorily as well, a full public service is expected to follow.

British Columbia Telephone (BCT)

British Columbia Telephone has been planning a field trial of the Telidon videotex system to take place in Vancouver. A starting date of late 1980 has been proposed. Around 150 participants are expected in the business, residential and closed user group sectors. By the end of 1979 the number and nature of the information providers was still undecided. The nature of the services to be offered was still under consideration, with security monitoring and energy management thought to be particularly likely.

Ontario Education Communications Authority (OECA)

The OECA has been planning a composite experiment involving four separate trials. The first is a broadcast Telidon teletext trial on TV Ontario educational network transmissions. The second is a Telidon videotex trial with a 10,000 page database in Toronto. Thirdly, OECA will participate in the Bell Vista trial. The fourth trial will be cable-based, run in conjunction with a major cable operator.

Up to 50 terminals were scheduled for placement in homes, educational institutions and secondary schools. OECA's objectives are non-commercial. Its aim has been to explore the potential of videotex in education, and to examine the opportunities for using videotex as a learning aid in homes. The trial information will be educational in nature, and it includes programme schedules by subject area, grade area and region, data of interest to school boards, computer based learning, and other applications.

Manitoba Telephone System's (MTS's) Ida

Project Ida has been described as a 'multi-faceted programme designed to test technology for the impending information age'. Both telephone and two-way cable TV services will be tested in the Ida programme, with a large number of applications including teleshopping, electronic mail and electronic funds transfer.

The telephone videotex part of the Ida project is planned to involve about 50 homes in the South Headingley, Winnipeg area, starting early in 1980. Initially, users should be able to access up to 10,000 pages of information, though this number will be increased if the demand is sufficient. A wide range of topics is expected to include stock quotations, local history, recipes and video games. Several newspapers will be information providers to the Ida test. They include the Winnipeg Free Press, the Winnipeg Tribune and the Toronto Star. Two other information providers are Infomart and Canadian Home Information Systems (CHIS).

Infomart is a company formed by Southam Inc. and Torstar Corporation (both information providers for Vista) as an umbrella for clients interested in becoming Telidon information providers. CHIS has described itself as an information broker, and was expecting to be an information provider to every Telidon field trial scheduled in Canada at the end of 1979. It will help individual information providers on technical matters, assisting with the design and preparation of data. It will also undertake page inputting and editing on behalf of clients.

CHAPTER 14

DEVELOPMENTS IN JAPAN

TELEPHONE-BASED VIDEOTEX

Japan began seriously to explore the alternative uses of television systems in the late 1960s—earlier than most other nations. This interest was an outgrowth of the Information Society programme, an ambitious national plan to advance Japanese society into the information age during the last three decades of the century.

Throughout the 1970s in Japan, high bandwidth cable attracted more interest as a delivery medium for community information services than narrow bandwidth voice grade telephone lines. Indeed, the information society programme has its roots at the time when interest in cable TV services was perhaps most euphoric.

Japan's two-way cable experiments, permitting residential users to access a wide range of services, have been well publicized. But they do not appear to have demonstrated conclusively either a universally enthusiastic response from residential users, or secure commercial prospects for service providers. They were, perhaps, both too ambitious and too expensive.

By the end of the 1970s, the relatively simple telephone based videotex concept was beginning to receive increasing attention. The most significant experiment at the time, called Captain, is described below. The leading cable experiments are described on the following pages.

Nippon Telegraph and Telephone (NTT) Captain

Captain (Character and Pattern Telephone Access Information Network) is a telephone based videotex system developed by NTT public corporation and sponsored by the Ministry of Posts and Telecommunications (MPT). A market trial was due to start towards the end of 1979. Around 1000 selected telephone subscribers, mainly residential, were to be connected in the Tokyo area.

The aim of the Captain trial is to evaluate operational, managerial and technical questions. A total trial budget of 3000 million yen ($13 million) has been assigned to cover the cost of development, installations, software and terminals.

At the start of the trial, the plan was for 100,000 pages of information to be available to cover topics including shopping, entertainment, sports information, news, education programmes and school entrance information.

By early 1979, MPT had organized an association of information providers with more than a hundred members from newspaper publishing, book and magazine publishing, advertising, travel and tourism, department stores, broadcasting and public bodies.

Users in the trial are expected to buy adapted TVs at a price representative of volume production. In addition, they appear likely to pay connect-time and page access fees on similar lines to the Prestel public service.

Fujitsu is responsible for the design and manufacture of the TV terminals. The terminals feature numeric keypads to permit users to select pages by numbered menu choice, or by direct page number entry from printed indexes. There are eight display colours, including black and white. The terminals are designed to display Japanese characters: Kanji, Hiragana and Katakana. The written language is characterized by a relatively large number—over 3000—of complex characters.

The character and graphic information making up individual page displays is stored at the Captain centre, and assembled for transmission as packets, one packet for each character block. Character blocks each contain a dot pattern which is a facsimile of the character, together with coded data specifying character attributes such as colour, background, and still/flashing. This contrasts with the European approach where information is stored and transmitted in coded form, with decoding and character generation carried out at the terminal. Had a similar approach been adopted for Captain, the decoding and character generation arrangements within each terminal would have been particularly complex.

The display grid is 8 rows each of 15 character cells, giving a total of 120 character cells. Each cell is 16×24 (384) dots, and can be used to display either a large character in a matrix of 15×18 (this allows for inter-row and inter-character gaps), or four smaller characters each in a matrix of 7×9, or four graphic characters each of 8×12.

The display capacity is thus 120 large characters or 480 small characters. The total number of pattern dots on the display is about 50,000, inclusive of head and side margins. The memory requirement is 8 Kbytes.

Over 1000 bits can be transmitted in a character block packet. Even at a relatively fast centre-to-terminal transmission rate of 4800 bits per second, full frames can take up to 30 seconds to build on a screen. The average is significantly less than this, around 10–15 seconds. Even so this is two to three times as long as with Prestel or Antiope.

Fujitsu's Davins

Davins is an extension of the Captain concept. It is being developed by Fujitsu using government research funds.

Davins (Data and Video Information Network System) is a videotex system which permits adapted TV terminals to be connected to information databases either through the telephone network or by cable. Increased flexibility compared with Captain was a design goal. The first Davins TV terminals had 64 Kbit memories. The expectation was for memories of 256 Kbits by 1982 or 1983.

The display grid is either 8 rows of 14 large characters each, or 24 rows of 42 small characters each. Large characters are defined with a 15×18 dot matrix, and small characters with a 5×7 dot matrix. Davins can display the same colours as Captain. The time to build a page display is claimed to be much faster, however—around 4 seconds on average.

Nippon Telegraph and Telephone (NTT) VRS

VRS (Video Response System) is a private venture videotex-like system which has been under development since 1973. NTT has been using it for internal experiments since the beginning of 1977, and has planned to sell it for private in-house use, and possibly even for public service before 1983.

Although VRS uses telephone lines to transmit information, it is significantly different in concept from both Captain and Davins. VRS uses separate lines to and from the TV terminal. The one bringing information to the terminal is a specially conditioned telephone line with a bandwidth sufficiently high to carry a full TV video signal of around 5 megahertz, together with audio. The conditioning is achieved by inserting repeaters into the line at frequent intervals.

The second line, from the TV terminal, is a regular telephone line. Its purpose is to permit users to contact the VRS centre in order to request services using either a special keypad attached to the terminal, or a separate telephone with a regular push-button dial.

The high bandwidth telephone line is plugged directly into the TV antenna socket. The TV does not have to be adapted as with other videotex systems.

The VRS service has been designed to transmit both static and moving video pictures together with audio. Because the TV terminals have no memory, the video information has to be transmitted continuously as in normal TV broadcasting. Still picture information is transmitted at a repetition frequency of 30 times per second.

During the late 1970s, the VRS system specification featured a capacity for 10,000 individual still picture frames, each consisting of character and graphic information in up to six colours as well as black and white.

TWO-WAY CABLE TRIALS

Tama New Town's CCIS

CCIS stands for 'Co-axial Cable Information Service', and is the name of the two-way cable experiment conducted among 500 selected households in Tama New Town in the suburbs of Tokyo.

The CCIS experiment is a joint venture by MITI (Ministry of Industrial Trade and Industry), MPT (Ministry of Posts and Telecommunications) and the Tama CCIS company formed especially for the purpose called VISDA (Visual Information System Development Association).

Tama was chosen as the site for the two-way cable experiment because it is a new town with systematic planning, and it has a representative cross-section of families in its total population of rather more than a quarter of a million residents.

The trial began in January 1976, and phase 1 was completed early in 1978. During this period ten quite different types of service were made available to samples selected from among the participants. Of these ten, one service, known as 'still picture request service', was a videotex type of service. It enabled still information stored at the service centre on microfiche to be selected by users through a keypad attached to the TV, and to be transmitted down the cable.

A selection of about 6000 pages of information was available on the still picture request service during normal hours, about 8.30 am until 9.30 pm. Of the 500 participants, 35 were equipped to use the service. The type of information available ranged from notices of community activities to recipes. Users requesting a transmission were able to receive a page in about 4 seconds on one of the TV channels.

Following the completion of phase 1, an analysis of the results concluded that only six of the ten services should be continued into a phase 2 trial period, to run into the early 1980s. The still picture request service was one of the chosen six, but the least popular of them. The other five were:
regular TV

original TV broadcasting	local community TV programmes
automatic repetition telecasting	a form of participative programme preparation
flash information	news, sport and weather forecast flashes superimposed on the regular picture
memo copy	for handwritten messages between users and the centre, and between users

160

The remaining four services were dropped for reasons of high cost and comparatively low popularity.

The response of the users equipped with the still picture request service was sampled over an 18 month period during phase 1. It showed a slowly growing perception of the advantages of the service. At the end of the period, about 40% of the users found it to be useful, about 40% of little use, and the remainder of no use.

A report issued at the end of phase 1 included an 'evaluation' by participants of all of the services. Apparently the still picture request service was not considered by participants to be worth more than about $2 per month.

Higashi-Ikoma Hi-OVIS

Like CCIS, Hi-OVIS is a two-way cable experiment offering a variety of services to householders. The outstanding feature of Hi-OVIS is its use of optical fibre cables in place of conventional co-axial copper cables. It is the first large scale two-way cable experiment of its kind in the world.

The Hi-OVIS experiment is being conducted through VISDA, under the guidance of MITI. A number of private industries are also involved including Fujitsu, Matsushita and Sumitomo.

The Hi-OVIS trial began in July 1978 with 168 participating households in Higashi-Ikoma New Town, in Nara Precinct. The experiment was planned to run for two years and to include a number of services, one of them being a still picture information service similar to the one in CCIS. It is based on microfiche like CCIS, and unlike Captain. The range of information available includes notices such as local news, local weather reports, and water and power shortages; local information guides such as doctors on duty during holidays, local facilities and events; and travel information such as road guides and railway timetables.

Hi-OVIS is a broad bandwidth system, like CCIS. Graphic and text images are transmitted down the cable using the full video bandwidth; data encoding is unnecessary. About 350 kilometres of optical fibre cable have been used to connect subscriber terminals via sub-centres to the Hi-OVIS centre.

Hi-OVIS is an ambitious and interesting project. But it is localized and heavily subsidized. Few private businesses in the USA or Europe would be prepared to undertake an equivalent experimental programme, with an investment cost reputedly as high as $40 million.

CHAPTER 15

CONCLUDING COMMENTS

Videotex is a simple, low cost, two-way information service able to use adapted TV terminals. A major emphasis is on information retrieval. With videotex, users can access large information databases through the regular telephone network. But the two-way capability of the telephone means that videotex can offer other services as well: computation, messages including purchase transactions and reservations, and software distribution.

Videotex is being developed in many countries, both within and beyond Europe. The potential rewards are attracting the attention of service providers worldwide. Although originally conceived primarily for the residential market, videotex is confronted there by the classic 'chicken and egg' problem. Its price is particularly volume sensitive. In the absence of subsidies or prolonged heavy investment, only large scale usage will ensure the low prices necessary to attract the mass residential market. The problem is how to generate the scale in the first place.

One answer lies in videotex's potential for the business market, which could become the catalyst for the investments necessary for growth in the residential market later. The features which make it potentially attractive to users at home appeal equally to business users—it is relatively inexpensive, easy to use and convivial. The business community has shown a great deal of interest, not only in publicly available videotex services, but in private closed user group and in-house operations as well.

For the next few years the market for videotex will have to be strongly encouraged by the suppliers, so the attitude of the industry sectors positioned to exploit videotex is important. It is an attitude which varies widely. Overall it is probably best described as being cautiously optimistic. Fundamental questions have yet to be answered, not only about the nature and extent of the emerging market sectors, but also about issues such as privacy, editorial responsibility and regulation.

The potential service providers are well aware of the risks as well as the opportunities. They are right to show caution over the timing and extent of their investments.

In Britain, the BPO has taken a risky and aggressive step in launching its publicly available Prestel service. Britain, perhaps surprisingly, had accumulated a greater wealth of experience with videotex by the end of the 1970s than any other country.

Prestel has encountered its share of difficulties. This is perhaps to be expected in view of the nature of the service and the amount of new ground which it breaks. As the world leader in videotex, at least at this time, Prestel has attracted a great deal of attention from other countries. It would be a mistake to assume the Prestel experience to be a reliable indicator of what may happen elsewhere; the findings are not necessarily transferable. Nonetheless, the fortunes of Prestel, whatever they are, will be important to other countries.

Prestel has been described as a first generation videotex system. Its wholehearted allegiance is to low cost and simplicity—both attributes of fundamental importance to the residential market. But these very attributes make it somewhat inflexible. And although an examination of Prestel's economics supports the view that at mass market levels, measured in hundreds of thousands, it should be available at prices which ordinary people might be prepared to pay, it will come under severe pressure from alternative TV-related devices competing for consumers' discretionary income.

Consequently in Britain the business community will be the lead-in market for videotex, in terms both of volume of terminals sold and usage. This is likely to be the case in other countries too. Both closed user group and in-house services will be important. Business usage of publicly available videotex will attract increasing interest often as a consequence of, rather than a precedent to, these private services.

The sales and usage of terminals in the residential market will follow business usage. Penetration of the residential market will begin with professional people and white collar workers—not the same demographic profile as caused the growth in colour TV in the late 1950s and 1960s. The professional and business people leading off the residential market will be better able to benefit from videotex and more prepared to pay for it. Many will already have experienced videotex in their places of work.

Usage in the residential marketplace will develop steadily as terminal prices drop. New users will include graduates from (more limited) teletext, and families with children for whom the educative content of the database will be a strong incentive. Others will be the small proportion of a national population dedicated always to acquire the latest device.

At first, the main application in both residential and business markets will be information retrieval. Typically the information will be volatile, compact and with a high momentary value—like business financial information, price comparisons and classified advertisements. As prices drop, the emphasis will move towards convenience; it will be easier to find out about things through videotex than through other sources. But videotex won't displace conventional information media—certainly not in the early 1980s anyway. Both will co-exist.

Following the information retrieval application, messages and software distribution will both become increasingly important. Message applications will include teleshopping, reservations and electronic mail. Software distribution will be important for small business systems and personal computers.

During the early 1980s, the markets for videotex will fragment. In each sector, videotex will meet different needs and different competition—some established, some new. It will be a period of very rapidly advancing progress in information technology. Advances will come from all sides: in storage, switching, transmission and display. A common ingredient will be falling hardware costs. Videotex itself will be just one of a number of new service spending opportunities vying for attention.

In the residential market, many of these new opportunities will be TV-related. But despite predictions that the TV will grow into an integrated home information centre, it is quite possible that the 1980s will see a divergence between entertainment and information services in the home. The TV's prime role may be to display information transmitted through cable, off-air, from video cassette recorders and videodiscs. Display terminals for videotex could begin to develop independently. In the home, such terminals may well be placed in the kitchen or hall rather than in the living room, which is the centre of home entertainment.

Whether or not this occurs, videotex terminals for the residential market will be characterized by increased intelligence, permitting local storage of multiple pages, manipulation of stored data and, in some cases, superior graphics. There will be a noticeable convergence between videotex terminals and personal computers designed for home use.

In the business marketplace, videotex will begin to converge with other electronic information services, particularly online retrieval systems and electronic mail.

Videotex will be just one element in the expanding spectrum of information systems. Conceivably by the mid-1980s it will be hard to identify videotex separately, and it may not even be sensible to try.

Videotex will be accepted, though perhaps not as rapidly or in quite the form that its protagonists have sometimes proclaimed. But with today's level of interest, it seems inevitable that it will become an accepted part of the everyday scene in the future.

GLOSSARY OF TERMS

Adapter	See decoder.
Alphageometric	Type of display able to show alphanumerics, and with the ability to build shapes from geometric instructions, e.g. PDIs.
Alphamosaic	Type of display able to show alphanumerics and coarse 'mosaic' graphic elements.
Alphaphotographic	Type of display able to show alphanumerics, and high resolution pictures of similar quality to normal TV video.
Analogue	The representation of numerical values by physical variables such as voltage, current etc. (contrasted with digital).
Antiope	The French standard for character coding and display on videotex terminals.
Asynchronous	Transmission in which each information character is individually synchronized, usually by the use of start and stop elements.
Autodialler	Facility to permit a terminal automatically to call a predesignated telephone number.
Autoidentifier	Facility permitting a terminal automatically to identify itself.
AVIP	Association of Viewdata Information Providers (British).
Bandwidth	The difference, in hertz, between the lower and upper limits of the wave frequencies that can be transmitted over a communications channel.
BBC	British Broadcasting Corporation, the state owned radio and TV broadcasting service.
Bildschirmtext	The West German PTT's videotex system.
Bit-map	See frame-store.
BPO	British Post Office, the British PTT.

165

BREMA	British Radio Equipment Manufacturers' Association.
Bulk transfer	Transfer of a batch of data in a continuous burst using a direct link between computers, or by magnetic tape transfer.
Bundespost	The West German PTT.
Captain	Character and Pattern Telephone Access Information Network—a Japanese videotex system.
CATV	Correctly 'community antenna TV' though commonly accepted as meaning 'cable TV'.
CCETT	Centre Commun d'Etudes de Télévision et de Télécommunications, the French PTT and TDF joint research establishment.
CCITT	Comité Consultatif International Téléphonique et Télégraphique, a worldwide representative body of PTTs and telephone service operators.
Ceefax	The BBC's broadcast teletext service.
Centre Operator	The organization responsible for running a videotex centre.
Character generator	A method of displaying characters on a display screen where the shapes of all possible characters are predefined and stored in the terminal's memory.
Chip	Abbreviation for silicon chip—a microelectronic device in which all the components are miniaturized and formed on a silicon chip.
Circuit-switched	The establishment of a communications channel by exchange switching techniques.
Closed user group	A service to which only predefined users have access.
C set	Control set, represented by 32 seven-bit characters.
CUG	Closed user group.
Database	A collection of data held in a machine-readable form, typically on magnetic discs.
Data network	Telecommunications network built specifically for data transmission, rather than voice transmission.
DataVision	The Swedish PTT's videotex system.
Decoder	A device used to decode videotex signals and display them on a TV screen.
Didon	The French broadcast teletext system, using the Antiope standard.

Download	To transmit information (especially software) down the line from a central store to a terminal.
Duplex	A communications channel permitting transmission in both directions simultaneously.
Editing terminal	The terminal used by an IP to input data into a videotex system.
Electronic mail	A mail service using electronics and telecommunications substituting for the regular physical mail.
End pages	The pages at the end of a tree structured database containing information. See also routeing page.
ESC	Escape, the control code transmitted to permit alternative meanings to subsequent codes.
Facsimile	A system for the transmission of printed images.
Floppy disc	A flexible disc with a magnetic surface typically holding a quarter of a million characters.
Focus group	A selected group possessing specific socio-economic attributes used for market research purposes.
Frame	A screenful of videotex information.
Frame-grabber	The logical element of a broadcast teletext decoder that captures a predesignated frame as it is broadcast.
Frame-store	A technique for displaying videotex information where each picture element of the frame is defined in the terminal memory.
GEC	General Electric Company, the British company whose 4000 series minicomputers are used for Prestel and other Prestel-based videotex systems.
Graphical primitives	A set of instruction codes transmitted to a terminal defining basic graphical shapes (circle, line etc.).
Gresham Street	The BPO office in London at which the Prestel Test Service computer centre is based.
G set	Graphics set, represented by 96 seven-bit characters, used to define the codes for display character shapes.
Host computer	A computer and associated database which, although run as separate entities, can be accessed via a network.
HTC	Helsinki Telephone Company.
Hz	Hertz, a measure of frequency (1 Hz = 1 cycle per second).

167

IBA	Independent Broadcasting Authority, the regulatory body controlling independent broadcasting in the UK.
In-house	(videotex system or service). A system for use only within a particular company or organization, where the computer centre is independent of any public service.
Insac	The British firm acting as the overseas agent for Prestel.
Interlace	For TV displays, the interleaving of the two separately transmitted fields.
IP	Information Provider.
ISO	International Standards Organization.
Jack socket	The telephone connection into which a videotex receiver (or decoder) is plugged.
Kanji	Japanese writing using Chinese characters.
Keyword	(search). Retrieval of information matching free text descriptors.
Line isolator	An electrical barrier to protect the telephone network from the high voltages in a terminal.
LSI	Large scale integration, the process of engraving many thousands of electrical circuits on a small chip of silicon.
Luminance	Amount of light emitted from a surface in a given direction.
Modem	Modulator/demodulator. Converts a digital signal to a signal suitable for telephone transmission and vice versa.
Multiplexor	A device to interleave or concurrently transmit more than one message on a single channel.
NTSC	National Television Standards Committee standard for colour television broadcasting in North America.
Offline	Mode of operation in which terminals, or other equipment, can continue to operate whilst disconnected from a central processor. Contrasted with online.
Online	Mode of operation in which terminals, or other equipment, are controlled by a central processor. Contrasted with offline.
Oracle	Broadcast teletext service operated in Britain by the IBA.
Packet	An addressed data unit of convenient size for transmission through a network.

Packet-switched	A technique for transmitting data packets through a network.
PAD	Packet assembler/disassembler, a device for attaching non-packet-mode terminals to a packet-switched network.
Page	The smallest unit of videotex information which can be addressed directly via the keypad. A page may consist of one or more frames.
PAL	Phase alternate line, one of two European standards for colour television broadcasting.
Parity	A system of adding a check bit to a string of bits to make the sum of all the one bits odd or even (hence parity bit).
Password	A (secret) identification number keyed by the user and checked by the system before permitting access to the database.
PDIs	Picture description instructions, containing graphical primitives.
Pel	Picture element, the smallest individual element that can be illuminated on a display screen.
Port	Access path into a computer system. For videotex systems the number of ports determines the number of simultaneous users.
Portable	For software, the property of being able to run programs without any changes on different hardware.
Protocol	The rules governing how two pieces of equipment communicate with one another.
PSTN	Public switched telephone network.
PTT	Post and Telecommunications authority.
RAM	Random access memory.
Raster	Set of television scan lines defining the picture.
Resolution	For a display terminal the number of picture elements into which the display can be resolved.
ROM	Read only memory.
Routeing page	A videotex display of routeing information.
Scan line	The horizontal lines on the surface of a TV tube.
SECAM	One of two standards for colour television broadcasting in Europe, developed in France.
SI	Shift in.
Sign-on procedure	To connect with a remote computer, including the provision of identification details and security access.
SO	Shift out (see also System Operator).

Socio-economic group	Classifications by job or occupation for market research purposes.
SS2 (or 3)	Single shift 2 (or 3).
Synchronous	For transmission, the sending and receiving instruments operate continuously at the same frequency.
System operator	The body responsible for the provision of a videotex service.
TDF	Télédiffussion de France, the state monopoly broadcasting company.
Télématique	Term coined in France to describe the combination of computers with telecommunications.
Telesoftware	Transmission (or broadcasting) of software for capture by an intelligent videotex terminal.
Teletel	In France, the name of the planned public videotex service.
Teletex	Super-telex system planned by European PTTs for the 1980s.
Teletext	A generic term for one-way broadcast information services.
Telidon	The Canadian Department of Communications' videotex system.
Telset	The videotex service developed in Finland.
TRANSPAC	French packet-switching network.
Tree structure	Arrangement of a database in a number of hierarchical levels, each lower level presenting information of increasing detail.
Umbrella IP	IP providing services to other IPs.
VBI	Vertical blanking interval, between TV field transmissions when the picture forming beam returns from the bottom to the top of the picture.
VCR	Video cassette recorder.
VDU	Visual display unit.
Videodisc	A disc containing prerecorded information for displaying on a TV screen.
Videogram	Generic term for devices for playback of pre-recorded material on a TV screen.
Wideband	High bandwidth.